PRAISE FOR
GrowUp

"The most important job of the founder is to establish a team that can scale the project. Coordinating the work of committed people isn't the same as doing the work yourself, and this book helps entrepreneurs find the useful path forward."

— **Seth Godin**,
Author *This is Marketing*

"Brilliant. Michelle deeply cares about founders; she has worked with many, some who have succeeded, and some who have not. In this inspiring and useful book, she shares an approach for founder self-awareness and how to act on it. If you are looking to take your startup to the next level and aren't sure how, I highly suggest reading *GrowUp* immediately."

— **Jim Stengel**,
CEO The Jim Stengel Company, Host of the CMO Podcast,
Author of *Grow*, Former Global Marketing Officer,
Proctor and Gamble

"Michelle Denogean's take on the four founder superpowers is spot on. At Matrix Partners, we have seen them all, both their strengths and blind spots. Her GROW system not only makes complete sense but is vital for every startup founder to embrace as they scale."

— **Dana Stalder**,
Partner, Matrix Partners

"*GrowUp* is spot on and, frankly, a must-read for every founder looking to build a long-lasting business that creates meaningful value. I've seen first-hand how Michelle's expertise and deep empathy for founders impacts startups' success. Her unique experience as a trusted sounding board for many founders throughout her career has given her the ability to create critical tools and frameworks to help even more companies accelerate growth."

– **Greg Sands**,
Founder & Managing Director, Costanoa Ventures

"Scaling a startup requires the right team to compliment your strengths as a founder. Michelle not only understands this deeply, but encourages founders to look within themselves and identify the growth needed to empower their teams for long term success."

– **Andy Moss**,
Founder & CEO at Mindtrip, former CEO and
Founder of the following: Roadster, Shopstyle, Fabkids

"Michelle's practical approach to maturing a growing company is essential for founders who want to maintain their authenticity while they scale their business."

– **Guy Gal**,
CEO of Side

"*GrowUp* is a must-read for startup founders looking to take their company to the next level by improving their own mindset. I wish I had this eight years ago when I started Luxury Presence!"

– **Malte Kramer**,
CEO Luxury Presence

"It's a hard truth: what makes founders great when they start isn't what makes them great as their companies grow. I've seen all the founder superpowers—and blind spots—Michelle calls out. Her GROW system is a pragmatic, hands-on roadmap for any founder wanting to become a better leader."

— **Martina Lauchengco**,
Partner, Costanoa Ventures
Author of *LOVED*

"If you are looking for a mirror in which to look at yourself and the company you've built, *GrowUp* is it. Michelle provides the perfect framework for CEOs and founders to ensure that they consider all the strengths and weaknesses of their organizations. Most important, she shines a bright light on blind spots that are likely holding you back from effectively scaling your company. I have worked with Michelle Denogean for many years. She has an innate ability to see the strengths and blind spots one cannot see in themselves. Read this book and let her help you scale and prosper!"

— **Rudi Thun**,
COO Mindtrip

"*GrowUp* is the first book of its kind to focus on the founder's mindset. No one talks about the emotional rollercoaster of starting and scaling a company, but take it from me, it can be a wild ride! Michelle Denogean approaches this topic with directness and care, offering practical advice for the personal journey founders take when scaling their companies."

— **Tara-Nicholle Kirke**,
MA, Esq., Founder & CEO of SoulTour,
Author of *The Transformational Consumer*

"Starting a company is one thing, scaling it for growth is quite another. The innovative strengths of a founder are altogether different from the leadership strengths needed to guide a startup from scale-up to grow up. This book should be required reading for any founder hoping to make those leaps successfully."

– Matthew E. May,
ScaleUp Strategist, Insight Partners, and co-author,
What a Unicorn Knows: How Leading Entrepreneurs Use Lean Principles to Drive Sustainable Growth

"Michelle offers an excellent guide and framework for business growth, drawing on her wisdom of someone who has experienced a significant transformation. The highlight is its focus on the internal journey, approached with great empathy and care."

– Kevin Eyres,
Conscious Leadership Coach, Teacher, and Speaker
and Former Managing Director, LinkedIn Europe

"To say I am inspired is an understatement. Michelle knows her subject matter and approaches the topic of business growth with genuine care and perceptive guidance. Anyone reading this book will have a proven path to follow as they grow their own business. I've been fortunate to start two businesses and work with founders of many others. Without question, I could have used this book to accelerate and ensure greater success. It will be at the top of my recommended list, and I'll use it as a workbook when helping others. Bravo!"

– David Kain,
President Kain Automotive

"Scaling a business is very different from starting one. Michelle Denogean not only understands this deeply but encourages founders to look within and identify the growth necessary to make their company successful long term."

— **Dawn Callahan**,
CMO Boingo Wireless

"The GROW framework is a founder's compass for identifying their superpower and leveraging it to lead their nascent endeavor to success. Michelle simplifies the complex struggle that comes along with being a founder-led startup into a consumable framework that positions leaders to lead with their strengths first. Her years of experience successfully guiding founders to find scale with their businesses and incredible strength as a people leader and storyteller make *GrowUp* a must-read!"

— **Stephen Capezza**,
President, Side

"*GrowUp* is an easy-to-read, idea-rich book that provides an excellent framework for founders to use in crafting their strategy and building their team. A must for every aspiring founder, whether a new graduate or someone launching a venture later in life."

— **Christopher Norris**,
Executive Director, Ciocca Center for Innovation and Entrepreneurship; Executive Director, Sustainable Business Institute; Adjunct Faculty, Leavey School of Business, Santa Clara University

Grow UP

TAKE YOUR STARTUP TO THE NEXT LEVEL

MICHELLE DENOGEAN, CMO

BERRY POWELL PRESS

GrowUp: Take Your Startup to the Next Level
Copyright © 2024 by Michelle Denogean

First paperback edition July 2024
Cover Design: Ari Kushimoto, Kay McConnaughey
Illustrations and Interior Design: Kay McConnaughey
Copyediting: Valeri Mills Barnes

Published by Berry Powell Press
Glendora, California
www.berrypowellpress.com

ISBN: 978-1-957321-18-9 (Paperback)
ISBN: 978-1-957321-19-6 (ebook)
Library of Congress Control Number: 2024911508

CONTENTS

**PART IV: What Practical Strategies Are Needed for
     Your Company to Thrive?**

This book is dedicated to my husband AJ and kids, Cody and Quinn, who ate a very late breakfast every weekend for over two years as I obsessed over the writing of it.

ACKNOWLEDGMENTS

I want to thank the countless founders and the leadership teams I have worked with over the years for letting me into their lives to help them grow their companies and for the opportunity to reference many of you in this book. In no particular order—Andy Moss, Guy Gal, Brandon Cavalier, Kevin Eyres, Jim Stengel, Rudi Thun, Matt Wolfe, Lisa Macnew, Amit Chandarana, Gannon Giguiere, Tara Nicholle Kirke, Suzanne Nagel, Dawn Callahan, and Malte Kramer, to name a few.

In particular, I thank Andy Moss and Rudi Thun, who opened my eyes to the fact that I am much more than a Marketing Executive in my contributions. That was the leap I needed to transform this book from a marketing book to what I am most passionate about—scaling businesses.

To my parents, Linda and Philip Gardner, who, despite their best efforts to get me into business from the get-go, supported my creative journey and allowed me to find my path into the business world. Yes, Dad, P&Ls are part of accounting, and I am good at it. I would also like to thank my publisher, Carmen Berry of Berry Powell Press, for believing in me and the concept behind this book. Carmen, you were more than a book publisher to me—not only were you an incredible author coach, but you allowed me into Berry Powell Press in such a way that we were able to build the book and apply it to the publishing company throughout the process.

I also want to thank Valeri Mills Barnes, my publishing coach, copy editor, and devoted cheerleader. Your contribution to this effort was profound. The entire team at Berry Powell Press deserves my gratitude, particularly Kay McConaughey, who drew the inside illustrations and designed the interior layout, and Carolyn Rafferty, the Director of Publishing, who pulled it all together and made it a book. I also want to highlight the amazing work of Ari Kushimoto, who designed my book cover, and Sophia Zey, who built my associated website. You both are incredible artists and, more importantly, lifelong friends.

Writing a book has been a bucket list item since I was twelve years old—so not only do I thank my twelve-year-old self, but also the teaching assistant in the Literature Writing program at UCSD who told me I would never write a book if I was working full-time. It might have taken me thirty years, but I did it.

INTRODUCTION

I wrote this book with one person in mind—you, the founder of a new business venture. Whether you are starting your very first company, are a few years into running your business, or are already on to your second or third company at this point, you have the startup bug. You're an entrepreneur at heart.

You know what I am talking about. The giddiness you get every time you talk about your vision. You have a strong point of view on the world and have identified a significant problem worth solving. In fact, you're convinced that the product you've created or the service you'll provide is big enough and better than what's out there now. What you have is what customers need precisely. Not only will you impact their lives, but your company will also make an addition to your pocketbook. It's an exciting dream, and you're all in. The one thing all founders have in common is that they are *incredible* at starting their businesses.

So why am I writing this book for you? After all, you're starting a company, and I acknowledge that you're terrific at achieving that goal. Let me introduce myself and explain why my message is essential to your long-term success.

My name is Michelle Denogean, and I have worked with dozens of startups and their founders across diverse industries, such as travel, real estate, automotive, online dating, ad technology, charitable giving, book publishing, and more. For over a decade, I have been part of the executive team, so I have a unique perspective on the founders' psyche and the decisions made along the way. I have seen their companies start up, struggle, and grow to their full potential.

I have worked with entrepreneurs like you and have discovered that many get stuck in the startup phase and have difficulty reaching sustainability. It can feel like you're driving your car at full speed, fueled by initial success, and then, out of nowhere, a brick wall appears. And there you are, as if suspended in time, wondering what to do next. Can you swerve fast enough? Is it possible to fly over it? Or will you lose control and smash into the wall, ending your dream in a tangled mess by the side of the road?

The sad truth is that most startups don't get past this wall. According to the Bureau of Labor report, Survival of Private Sector Establishments by Opening Year, twenty percent of startups close their doors within twelve months of opening their businesses. The longer a company is in business, the steeper the odds. By year two, thirty percent fail; by year five, nearly fifty percent of startups call it quits. Some companies hang on for a time, but eventually, ninety percent of startups never make it past the startup phase. (startupgenome.com, Global Startup Ecosystem Report 2019)

Why did it feel like the world was your oyster in the very beginning? Why were you so successful at the onset, only to find yourself waking up each morning worried that you might not meet this month's payroll? Is it possible that after all you and your team have invested in starting this new dream company, it won't be sustainable in the long run? Is there a dark cloud looming over your head that causes you to question yourself and the dream you're pursuing?

I wrote this book for you, the founder, so you won't be surprised by the many small and large walls that will appear along your company's journey. Instead, you will be well prepared for what is ahead. I want you to be part of the ten percent who know how to navigate the road between a startup and a scalable, sustainable company. And if you already see a massive wall on the road ahead, my program will provide you with the understanding and strategies needed to be one of the ten percent who GrowUp.

What makes my approach different from the thousands of business books published every year declaring to have *the* answer for success? How can I claim to have the missing piece to your puzzle, especially when I have yet to be a founder? These are essential concerns for me to address to establish my credibility.

First, in addition to my C-suite experience as a marketing executive, I have held operating roles in product development, operations, and analytics for over twenty years. As a result, I have a unique perspective across industries and the roles and personalities of people who have filled these seats around me.

Second, I have hands-on experience helping build startups. I have had a birds-eye view of some succeeding while others failed. I've seen what outsiders don't have access to and can pass this on to you while you are building your own company. You don't want to learn from someone who has only studied these topics academically. You want an expert who has boots-on-the-ground experience.

Third, ninety percent of founders themselves don't always see the problem. I've spent a great deal of time observing and studying entrepreneurs in action. I am someone who can take an honest look at how the founder's strengths and weaknesses impact the organization at large. Would you trust another woman to deliver your baby just because she had a baby herself? Or would you turn to a doctor who may not have given birth but has experienced the different scenarios that can come up in the delivery room?

The truth is, I care deeply about the founders that I have worked with, many of whom I have deep relationships with to this day. Some have even gone on to start second or third companies, often turning to me for advice along the way. My relationships with founders hold a special place in my heart. They inspire me with their vision and willingness to throw caution to the wind and jump into the fire with both feet. Their internal drives and motivations for making things happen without guarantees gobsmack me. Yet, I have seen these same individuals struggle when their companies no longer look like the dreams they once started. When that fire in their bellies starts to burn down, I have seen the walls they hit and the gut punch it causes when they need to navigate around it. It can be brutal.

This book is my way of giving back and massively reaching startup founders with my support. You can and will survive this business phase, but it does require reflection and an openness to change.

How can the majority of talented, intelligent, creative, and dedicated people who could get a new and novel company rolling end up having to close their doors? There must be a common mistake that ninety percent of founders are making. I have discovered the answer to that conundrum.

This book provides a unique framework that will equip and empower you to become the leader your company needs to grow. You'll gain new insight into your strengths and points of vulnerability. *GrowUp* is filled with examples of real business mistakes and triumphs, as well as composite stories so that you can find yourself on the pages.

The first few years of building your startup are blissfully dependent on your actions as the founder. But there is always a nagging concern that sits in the background. One that you may be experiencing right now is: "Do I have what it takes to scale this company? Will what makes me great as a founder now be what it takes to make my company great as it grows?" Here's the straight truth—what makes you great at starting will not make you great at growing. Most founders intuitively know this truth, but few understand what this truly means. Because who you are as a founder plays a massive role in how your company will grow.

The most beneficial wisdom you'll find will be deeper self-awareness and how to work more effectively with your team and customers. If applied correctly, my model will help your company join the ten percent of startups that make it. *GrowUp* is more than a book. It is a system that founders need to deploy to go from a successful startup to a fully scaled and grown-up company.

> **"**
> Here's the straight truth: What makes you great at starting is not going to make you great at growing.

Every founder's challenges are unique, so you may find that not every chapter is applicable to your current situation. That is totally fine. Feel free to skip around.

However, please take the time to read the first section of this book in detail, even if you don't identify with that type of founder.

Spoiler alert—this is going to be an empowering experience. So, hold on to your hats and glasses because the beginning of this book requires a lot of self-reflection before you even start the journey of scaling your business to the next level. Get ready for it!

PART I

WHAT MADE YOUR STARTUP SUCCESSFUL AT THE START?

CHAPTER 1

What Is Your Superpower?

With great power comes great responsibility.
– Stan Lee

Not everyone is cut out to be an entrepreneur—but you are. Not everyone starts a company from scratch—but you have. Not everyone's startup is successful—but yours has started great.

As an operator and a business consultant, I've worked with founders who have produced incredible success in the early days of their companies. They have described this experience as exhilarating, almost magical, and affirming. I don't mean to imply that it was easy. No, starting a company took a lot of hard work and long hours, but their dreams became reality.

Motivated by high goals and bolstered by the initial triumph, founders often share an attitude of excitement, even to the point that they may feel invincible. They do what comes naturally to them, and it works because every successful founder has what I call a Startup Superpower.

> **"**
> Every successful founder has what I call a Startup Superpower.

A Startup Superpower is the *one thing* you do best. You may not know you have this Superpower because it comes easily and naturally to you. But others notice this about you, whether or not you are mindful of it. This Superpower comes from your unique personality traits and the inner strengths you possess.

You might think I'm overly dramatic in calling what you do well a Superpower, but I think it's the right term. I'm not talking about having a "skill set" or something resulting from years of experience. Rather, I'm referring to the way you see the world and what's important to you at your deepest core—how your brain works. You don't have to think about exercising your Superpower because it's a natural expression of *who you are.*

Because it's so fundamental to your personality and the choices you make, you may take your Superpower for granted. You might not even recognize that you have a Superpower. But it would be a mistake not to realize just how this Superpower has been the foundation for your startup's initial success.

What Is a Superpower?

According to Wikipedia, a Superpower is a special or extraordinary superhuman ability greater than what is considered normal. While primarily discussed in science fiction stories as a key attribute of superheroes, the term can be applied to people generally. For this book's purposes and for business leaders in particular, a Superpower is the unique ability or skill someone brings to the team that most people have not mastered.

The Four Types of Superpowers

I've identified four different types of Superpowers that successful entrepreneurs embody. They are:

1. The power to Innovate
2. The power to Build
3. The power to Connect
4. The power to Persuade

Founders may have some strengths in all four of these Superpowers, but most have one Superpower, their primary way of being in the world. Pay attention to the following statement:

A company can successfully launch based on the founder's Startup Superpower. But a company cannot GrowUp without having a team in which all four Superpowers are actively engaged.

And what about the ten percent that do survive? Consciously or intuitively, this small group of founders realize that their company can't grow based solely on their single Superpower. They have to expand their vision and bring in the strengths, perspectives, and brilliance of the other three Superpowers.

This revelation might seem too simple, but I want to reiterate that ninety percent of companies fail because the founders don't see beyond their point of view. This concept will all be explained, step by step, in this book.

So let's start at the beginning and focus on discovering what your personal Superpower is and how it has taken you as far as you've come already. I've developed a Superpower Quiz so that you can dig deeper into what has made you so successful thus far.

Superpower Quiz

Before you take the quiz, I want to acknowledge the significant contribution that Carl Jung and those who have built upon his work have made to creating my GrowUp Model. The Superpower quiz is based on the Myers-Briggs Type Indicator inspired by Jung's work. This type of assessment is often used in business settings, so you might have taken it before. If so, you will recognize the initials used in the quiz. I have found it extremely valuable when consulting with companies that are struggling with challenges.

At the same time, I want to state that I have no formal or informal affiliation with, nor is my model endorsed by, the creators of the Myers-Briggs Type Indicator.

The GrowUp model is not a "scientific" tool in the sense that it measures reliable data. The accuracy of this quiz is based solely on your answers. It is not empirically accurate nor to be interpreted as a "diagnosis" of any kind. Your scores may change over time or if you imagine yourself in different contexts. So, I offer this simply as a tool that focuses on the traits of entrepreneurs who have started companies. Please select the answer that fits most closely with how you operate as a leader.

You may find that you are on the fence with some questions. Choose the answer (A or B) that has an edge over the other one.

Want to take the Superpower Quiz online?
Scan the QR code below.

	Please place a "1" in either the A or B column for each question below.	A		B	
1	Do people you work with describe you more as...	Realistic			Imaginative
2	When making decisions, are you more likely to...	Carefully consider the facts			Go with what feels right
3	Would you rather be known for your...	Sensibility			Creativity
4	Do you make your decisions based on the...	Principle			Circumstance
5	Great leaders are people who...	Are direct and clearly describe their vision			Use metaphors and analogies
6	The best teams are more likely to...	Get down to business			Have friendly banter
7	What gives you the most satisfaction?	A sales report			Conversations with customers
8	When providing feedback to your employees, is it more important to be...	Truthful			Tactful
9	When evaluating options, do you start with...	Objective input			Gut instinct
10	Would you rather help your team...	Make logical decisions			Trust their experience
11	Are you more interested in hearing about...	Details			Ideas & possibilities

12	Would you rather be described as...		Cool-headed		Warm-hearted
13	Do you prefer to learn from...		An expert		Experiment on your own
14	What do you prioritize more?		What needs to be done		The welfare of others
15	What do you think about dreamers? Are they...		Unrealistic		Fascinating
16	Would you rather talk about your...		Ideas		Observations
17	When starting a project, do you first...		Organize it step by step		Look at the big picture
18	When it comes to reprimands, do you prefer to be seen as...		Just		Merciful
19	Would you feel more discouraged if you were told your idea...		...isn't supported by the data		...lacks imagination
20	Would you rather have your team see you as...		Prepared		Inspiring
21	When you are trying to make a point, do you...		Recite facts you believe to be true		Describe patterns you see
22	Would you feel worse if something you said was...		Inaccurate		Hurtful
23	If you had an hour to spare, would you use it to...		Read an article with the latest research		Brainstorm new ideas
24	Would you prefer to have an employee who is...		Diligent		Dedicated

Use the table below to tally your answers. Place a check mark next to the answer (A or B) that you selected in the quiz above for each question. Count how many check marks you have selected per column and place that number in the TOTAL box at the bottom of the chart. Pay attention to the corresponding letter underneath your total per column as you will need that in the scoring section that follows. If your answers are close in any one category, you may have components of multiple Superpowers at play.

Scoring Chart

	A	B		A	B
1			2		
3			4		
5			6		
7			8		
9			10		
11			12		
13			14		
15			16		
17			18		
19			20		
21			21		
23			24		
Total					
	S	N		T	F

Scoring

Let's assess the superpowers in order of your strengths.

Step One:
Put your total number for each letter (S, N, T, F) in the boxes below.

Step Two:
Add up the numbers to the right and place in Total column. The highest score identifies your Superpower.

Step Three:
Identify the order of your strengths in Order column with 1 being the highest and 4 being the lowest.

Superpower	Sensate: S	Intuitions: N	Thinking: T	Feeling: F	Total	Order
Innovator	■			■		
Builder		■		■		
Connector		■	■			
Persuader		■	■			

Write the names of the Superpowers with 1 being the highest and 4 being the lowest.

1. _____=Your Primary Superpower
2. _____
3. _____
4. _____

Here's an Example:

Our hypothetical founder had the following scores:
S: 2 **N:** 10 **T:** 7 **F:** 5

Superpower	S	N	T	F	Total	Order
Innovator	■	10	7	■	17	1
Builder	2	■	7	■	9	3
Connector	■	10	■	5	15	2
Persuader	2	■	■	5	7	4

The Superpowers in order of scores for this example

1. Innovator (17) = Primary Superpower
2. Connector (15)
3. Builder (9)
4. Persuader (7)

Let's look at your numbers

Each letter has a maximum of twelve points. If your score is high in one area, that facet of your personality is strong. This is neither good nor bad news, for with every strength comes a weakness.

You may also have a tie between your N and S or T and F. This means your strengths are more evenly distributed. Again, this is neither good nor bad news. Every aspect of your personality has a counterpoint.

The Superpower Quiz Explained

Each question corresponds to different aspects of personality. There is no wrong answer and no "bad" Superpower. Every strength is needed, and every strength has a weakness. So, no matter where you land on the continuum, you're right where you ought to be.

Intuitive or Sensate: How Do You Perceive Reality?

Let's start with how you decide what is real. Those who are Intuitive (marked by the letter N) trust their intuition and go with their "gut" when assessing a situation. In contrast, Sensates (marked by the letter S) rely on data and facts and trust their five senses. Intuitives see the world according to patterns, see connections between events and ideas, and are usually more forward-looking. They wonder, "What could be imagined?"

Meanwhile, Sensates value "facts" that can be proven or disproven through observation or logic. These are the scientists, researchers, and fact-checkers. They ask, "What is here and now?"

Intuitive Leaders (marked by the letter N) trust their intuition and go with their "gut" when assessing a situation. They see patterns in behaviors, trends, events, often making connections between events and ideas, and are usually more forward-looking. They wonder, "What could be imagined?"

Sensate Leaders (marked by the letter S) have their feet planted firmly on the ground and rely on data and facts gathered by their five senses. They aren't swayed by emotional arguments or anecdotal examples. They are the scientists, researchers, and fact-checkers. They ask, "What is factual and reliable?"

Thinking and Feeling: What you believe is important and how you make decisions.

The other two letters are T for Thinking and F for Feeling, indicating how people determine what is important. Thinkers make decisions based on logical arguments. They emphasize law, justice, and fairness and tend to be more objective when applying standards. In contrast, Feelers make decisions based on their personal values. They tend to see the exceptions to the rule, are concerned with being merciful, and may be moved by emotions and anecdotal examples.

I am not fond of the terms that are used in the Myers-Briggs Type Indicator. Thinking people have feelings, and Feeling people are quite able to think. So, consider this when you interpret your scores. This continuum indicates what you believe is important, especially when it comes to making decisions.

Thinking Leaders (T) are logical and concerned with justice fairly applied to everyone. If you are a Thinker, you respect reasoning that follows the accepted laws of logic. Sentimental or emotion-based arguments rarely move you. The rules should be stated clearly, and everyone should be held equally accountable. Thinkers dispassionately make decisions. Certainly, no one should get "special" treatment.

Feeling Leaders (F), on the other hand, may value justice; they are more likely to see the exceptions to the rule. If you are a Feeler, you're quick to pick up on the feelings of others and empathize with them. While a Thinker is less likely to make decisions based on how people feel, this is of vital importance to you. You are invested in your relationships and want to maintain harmony, even if it means bending the rules.

Summary Chart

Superpower	To Innovate	To Build	To Connect	To Persuade
Characteristics	Intuition **(N)** Thinking **(T)**	Sensation **(S)** Thinking **(T)**	Intuition **(N)** Feeling **(F)**	Sensation **(S)** Feeling **(F)**
Founder	Innovator **(NT)**	Builder **(ST)**	Connector **(NF)**	Persuader **(SF)**

CHAPTER 2

The Four Superpowers

"The things that make us different, those are our superpowers." —Lena Waithe

Now that you know about the four superpowers, including the one that is your primary area of strength, we can dig in and understand each Superpower in more detail. It's natural for you to be most interested in the section on your Superpower. But please read about all four. As you read about other superpowers, be mindful of the traits you share and those you don't. Identifying your strengths and weaknesses is central to turning your startup into a sustainable success.

Note: The following fictional characters represent a compilation of people I have worked with and their associated experiences.

Superpower #1: The Power to Innovate
How can I solve my customer's problem in a new and innovative way?

Meet Jane. Jane is a big-picture person with the ability to look at what is and imagine what could be. She's about a year into launching her company based on an idea that occurred to her after observing struggling sales teams from small to mid-sized companies. She conceived of a way to automate much of the sales process, thereby increasing the potential sales of each team member while avoiding the need to bring on more support staff. Jane was confident that her idea would drastically improve sales efficiency even though it ran counter to the prevailing ideas in the industry.

Jane initially ran the idea by ex-colleagues in various sales organizations, and they raised some questions. Jane was prepared with the answers and helped them look at the problem and solution in a new way. Her enthusiasm and confidence were infectious, and their response was a delighted "Yes!"

They were excited about its potential, and many lined up to test her first iteration. She raised seed funding from family and friends—enough to bring on some initial employees: her founding team, people she had worked with in the past and could trust to help her make this dream a reality.

More importantly, her team was devoted and energized by Jane's vision. They poured everything into reaching out to new clients, ready to take a risk on such a ground-breaking concept. While what they had created at that point may not have been perfect, they now had a product that people could try, with many of her initial interviewees using it for free and providing feedback to improve as they grew.

Starting Point: Being a Problem Solver

Innovators like Jane are natural problem solvers who jump in with both feet once they find a big problem to solve. Yet, Innovators know it takes time to build solutions. They are very open and honest with customers about the many iterations their products or services may experience. As a result, they attract early adopters as their initial customers—people who love to be on the ground floor helping to shape the final offering. Jane's startup success is directly tied to her power to Innovate.

She's intuitive, solution-obsessed, charismatic, and driven, thriving on the power of ideas and the speed of innovation. She is well-spoken and has been the company's primary spokesperson from day one. She is often featured in the media and asked to present at conferences. Jane's talk track goes beyond what her company does. She is focused on transforming the industry, which means addressing important and timely topics whenever possible.

One of the most compelling aspects of the idea for Jane is that it challenges the status quo and the "normal" assumptions her industry has made about what would and wouldn't work. Innovators like Jane enjoy stirring things up a bit. There's a slight rebelliousness in Jane as she challenges old patterns of thought and sees herself as a changemaker, not only in the lives of her clients but the industry as a whole.

The Two Key Descriptors

The two words that best describe an Innovator are intuitive and logical. They see patterns and trust their gut reaction when faced with a challenge. However, they are also highly logical thinkers who can easily and quickly turn those intuitive insights into a product or service that solves a problem. As is typical for Innovators, Jane's enthusiasm and confidence are infectious, pulling people into her vision with the same passion she personifies.

People want to work with her and for her. Early customers are thrilled with the product, even if it needs some tweaking because they are enthralled with being on the ground floor of something new, different, and innovative. Think of Steve Jobs, perhaps the most influential Innovator in our lifetime.

Other Words that Describe an Innovator Are:

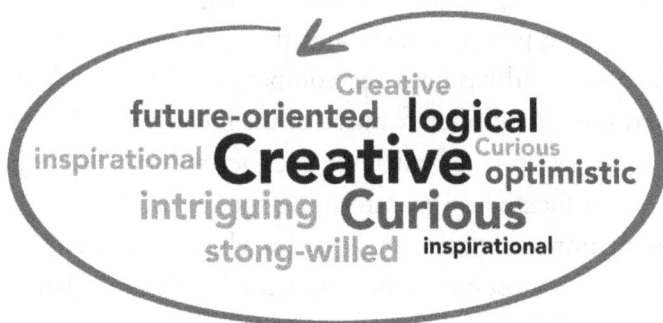

Innovators Are Masters at "Gaining Conviction"

Innovators' minds are idea-creating machines—constantly scanning for patterns, problems and potential breakthroughs. Due to the unique way that Innovators look at the business world, they instinctively focus on creating products and services that solve the problems many people experience. It comes naturally to try to improve the world around them. And with the desire to create a better future, they notice where things aren't working well. They are natural problem solvers.

"There's no shortage of remarkable ideas;
what's missing is the will to execute them." –Seth Godin

As a result Innovators come up with many ideas, some better than others. So they must ask themselves: *Which of my ideas are good ideas? Which of my good ideas are big enough to be lucrative? Which good idea has the most potential for me to create a successful startup?*

Successful Innovators don't act on their intuition alone to answer these critical questions. They are quite logical and collect information from the industry and others who know their potential buyers. Most importantly, Innovators talk to prospective customers to confirm that their solution will meet a need that people will buy.

But being savvy entrepreneurs, they realize that finding a sellable product isn't about placing confidence in what customers *say they want*; it's about identifying what they truly need, helping them to solve real problems, and, therefore, providing real value.

After doing thorough research and conducting interviews, Innovators carefully evaluate the information they have gathered. Some ideas, even their favorite ones, might not be as wonderful as the Innovator dreamed them to be. But being committed to investing in a successful endeavor, Innovators are fast on their feet and quickly pivot to an alternative vision that better hits the mark.

An Innovator who can launch a successful startup first relies on their ability to see patterns and make connections others may not see. Secondly, their ideas are rigorously examined until they are thoroughly convinced that their product will be the foundation for a viable business. This core competency is called "Gain Conviction."

> **"**
> Finding a sellable product isn't about what customers say they want, it's about identifying what they truly need.

The more people show excitement for the Innovator's ideas, the more conviction the Innovator has to push forward. With conviction, the Innovator pours their passion into making new ideas a reality. As a result, customers trust the Innovator and develop extreme loyalty for their products and company overall.

Innovation is not a one-and-done exercise at the company's onset. As the company grows, Innovators expand viable businesses by constantly re-evaluating and allowing evolution. Conversations with customers and observed behaviors keep the Innovator curious and inspired. As customer profiles change, the Innovator's ideas evolve. With each iteration, the level of confidence must be reassessed. Gaining conviction is a never-ending process.

Are You an Innovator?

If you are an Innovator, your Superpower has made you successful at starting your company because you have done your homework and have unwavering confidence in yourself and your ideas. You have gained conviction that your products or services will succeed in a competitive marketplace.

You know you see things that others overlook. Others may see a dead end while you recognize the door of opportunity. "Can't" isn't a dealbreaker but a dare to be taken and overcome. No mountain is too high to climb. Confident, passionate, and determined, as an Innovator, you will get over that mountain one way or the other, even if you have to fly.

Customers, weary of being frustrated by the challenge, are delighted to find someone like you who sees a new approach that aligns with their problems. Employees and customers know they have an opportunity that might pass them by if they hesitate to join you. You are going forward with this novel idea, with or without them. And enough people join you in the journey rather than be left behind.

> **Reflections:**
> - In what ways do you exhibit the traits of an Innovator?
> - What qualities of the Innovator do you wish to develop?
> - Are there elements of the Innovator that feel completely foreign?

Roadster: A True Story of a Successful Innovator

Roadster, a digital retailing platform for the automotive industry, was started by an Innovator named Andy Moss. Andy is a serial entrepreneur, so Roadster was not his first rodeo. Prior to Roadster, Andy founded ShopStyle, a popular fashion website that Rakuten eventually purchased.

Andy's Roadster adventure was born from one simple idea: If we know how to sell fashion online, even though we never thought we could, what other categories or industries have yet to transition to online sales that could benefit from an expedited online shopping experience? Andy's team made a list of options, and automotive reached the top.

There was one problem—despite his experience as a founder, Andy had zero experience in automotive. So, he waited to dive in. Instead, he started talking to people he knew about their experiences with buying cars. It turned out that almost everyone he interviewed hated the car dealership experience. Companies like Beepi were already trying to tackle e-commerce for used vehicles. Still, the greenfield opportunity—an opportunity no one else has pursued yet, was e-commerce for new cars.

Andy saw the opportunity but realized he needed an expert on staff who understood the car buying process. So, his next move was to find seed funding to purchase a small car brokerage in the San Francisco area called Buyside Auto. He studied the ins and outs of the car buying process, from inventory to pricing, financing, trade-ins, and protection plans. He spoke to customers on the car broker-age side of the business and watched the challenges and feedback they gave through their experiences. Andy, with his trusted software engineering team, began automating the experience the brokerage provided. They worked with local car dealerships to guarantee pric-ing and arrange vehicle delivery.

Andy's mission was to transform the car buying experience for new car buyers. With an NPS of ninety-five and hundreds of cars purchased on their platform, he did just that. (NPS is an acronym for Net Provider Score. It measures how well an organization builds loyal customer relationships.) And when he hit a roadblock trying to expand the company's operation to other markets, Andy knew it was time to pivot. He had already heard from several local car dealerships that they loved the platform and wished they could use it for their dealerships directly. Andy and his team quickly pivoted to provide software as a service to car dealerships across the country.

Superpower #2: The Power to Build

How do I build this company to ensure we are successful in the long term?

Meet Rich. Rich is in his third year of startup success. Like the Innovator, he is logical and strategic. Unlike the Innovator, however, he does not trust his intuition to make decisions. Rich may even roll his eyes at the Innovator for being a little too "pie in the sky" for his way of thinking. Builders like Rich rely on hard facts, research, and numbers. His goal is to build a strong foundation of policies, procedures, and a way to track successes and failures.

As a result, Rich has seen steady revenue growth each year he's been in business. He put processes in place early to ensure his team could track their growth and any declines in real time. He surrounds himself with the brightest talent available—people like him who are operationally savvy and can execute accordingly.

Data is of utmost importance to Rich. Barely a day goes by that Rich doesn't know precisely what the company has spent and earned. He has a line of sight on all key performance indicators necessary to accomplish their goals. Rich thoroughly enjoys a drama-free day with meetings held on time and challenges anticipated and confronted before problems have a chance to take hold.

Because Rich can show steady growth, he has been able to raise several rounds of funding over the past three years. He never raises more than he needs, but investors continue to invest because they believe in Rich's ability to make it happen.

Unlike the other startup founder types, Rich and his team are less likely to wear multiple hats because everyone has a clear job description and is expected to perform their duties effectively and efficiently. Sometimes, it may feel like the company runs itself;

things go so smoothly, but don't let this fool you. Rich is aware of everything that goes on in his company and is carefully monitoring and making minor but necessary adjustments daily. Employees focus on their respective areas, with Rich leading the helm, reviewing the data, and ensuring everything goes as planned.

Starting Point: Planning and Efficiency

Rich's startup success is highly dependent on his power to Build. He is a master at envisioning how each part of the company interacts with the others. He's also skilled in hiring staff that shares his values of order, outcomes, and predictability. Everything is measured with Rich, which means the company has a good handle on the input needed to get the desired output.

For Rich, a steady pace wins the race. His team sets goals, tests new strategies, and adjusts to accomplish them. He is proud of their progress, which he feels it is a good indicator of their ability to achieve the company's long-term goals.

Builders like Rich run a tight ship. They spend their time strategically with employees, reviewing progress and discussing modifications to current products, services, and processes to meet upcoming milestones.

The Two Key Descriptors

The two words that best describe a Builder are analytical and logical. Think Jeff Bezos—they delight in saying, "My company is efficient."

Other Words that Describe a Builder Are:

data and facts-driven
Process-focused **organized**
planful
systematic **Analytical** Dependable
predictable **Detail-oriented**
Action-oriented

Builders Are Masters at "Ramping Up"

Builders engage with the world of business from a down-to-earth, "let's be realistic" point of view. They are planners, first and foremost. They are like architects who design high-rise buildings from the ground up, ensuring that the foundation is sound enough to support the many floors of structure that will be built upon it. A Builder focuses on the company's foundation so the business can grow. This core competency is called "Ramp Up."

Builders live in the real world of balance sheets, sales reports, and the bottom line. As a result, they create orderly and predictable companies. Process and procedures are essential to measuring success.

Fiscal awareness and analytics are central to any successful Builder. Consequently, every initiative the company takes has an expected outcome and is measured and reported on appropriately.

Builders hire only the people they need when they are needed and build the operational systems and reporting mechanisms for those people to operate within. If the people they hire cannot meet the goals that are set out and measured, Builders act swiftly to replace them with people who can.

Raising money is a critical step in the process of growing a company. The Builder will shine at fundraising once all the proof points are gathered to show ongoing success. No one can showcase data and financial projections like the Builder. Whether asking friends and family during the seed stage or raising hundreds of millions of dollars to pour fuel into the rocket ship, raising money is a massive part of creating and sustaining a business.

Once fundraising is complete, no matter how much is raised, Builders spend judiciously. Sure, there are many things to spend money on, but Builders can directly attribute the right things to a desired outcome. They are thoughtful and methodical in their approach. They never spend money frivolously, resulting in them doing a great job at growing the business on a budget.

Are You a Builder?

If you are a Builder, your Superpower made you successful at starting because of your attention to detail. Everything your company rolls out is thoughtfully planned from start to finish. Your goals are clearly articulated, you track your metrics, your finances are in order, and you follow procedures. Customers find the solutions flawless and rave about your service levels to other prospective customers who may be interested in trying it out.

As a Builder, you attract doers to your organization. Hence, everyone feels accountable for producing results against their piece of the puzzle. They not only meet their goals, but they also report on them every step of the way. Your team culture is strong. Collectively, they thrive on hitting milestones, celebrating successes, and recognizing one another regularly. People join your organization, and investors provide funding because they believe that you have what it takes to Ramp Up to success.

Reflections:
- In what ways do you exhibit the traits of a Builder?
- What qualities of the Builder do you wish to develop?
- Are there elements of the Builder that feel completely foreign?

Amazon: A True Story of a Successful Builder

When you think of Amazon, you probably think of the innovation that *is* Amazon. After all, nobody was selling books online—let alone everything else under the sun—when Jeff Bezos came up with the idea. However, Jeff Bezos was not just an Innovator in the startup sense but also a Builder. Are you not convinced? Look at what Jeff was doing before Amazon. Jeff was running hedge funds on Wall Street and taking ballroom dance lessons to "increase the flow" of women in his life. He was an analyst at heart. (Founders, Senra, 2022)

In 1994, Jeff saw the Internet growing by twenty-three hundred percent in one year and knew he needed to be part of it. He listed things he could sell online and thought books were his best option. He modeled what this business could look like in five years before he spent a single minute building it. And the model that he originally built planned for slow growth, reaching profitability in year five.

When Jeff attempted to bring on investors, they were quickly disappointed about the speed of the company's growth. It wasn't fast enough to justify their investment, and they feared the company wouldn't survive long-term.

Boy, were they wrong. Within a month of launching, Amazon sold books to people in fifty states across forty-five different companies. As you know, the growth continued, and the company eventually went public in 1997.

What you may not know is that Amazon started with a culture of metrics and, to this day, tracks its performance against five hundred measurable goals. Jeff played a critical role in establishing this culture, which can also be seen in the processes he established early on. These include requiring six-page pre-reads before meetings and his two-pizza policy that keeps team sizes small to maximize their productivity. Process and efficiency are key characteristics of the Builder, and Jeff has those characteristics in spades.

Yet, Jeff is more than just a Builder at heart. His focus on courage, curiosity, and the customer makes him a unique hybrid of Innovator and Builder. According to Sydney Finkelstein, a Dartmouth University professor and the host of the business podcast *The Sydcast*, "What sets Bezos apart is how he balances his penchant for efficiency with the courage and curiosity central to everything he does." His belief in innovating versus following encouraged his team to focus on solving problems while ignoring the competition. He was customer-obsessed, even going so far as to leave an empty chair in meetings to represent the customer. While he was all about delegation, defining roles to reduce conflict, and empowering teams to make decisions, his extreme focus on putting the customer first makes him an Innovative Builder worth studying.

———

Superpower #3:
The Power to Connect
How many people can I get to believe in my cause?

Meet Sam. Sam is a few years into her startup journey and has spent most of her time building relationships with her startup team, customers, and others in the industry she serves. Sam is a Connector, creating a very different startup than an Innovator like Jane, even though both rely on their intuition. Jane focuses on the bigger picture of ideas, trends, and solving problems for large groups of people. In contrast, Sam uses her excellent intuitive skills to read people, strengthen relationships, and position her company in the industry. Sam makes her decisions in accordance with what is important to her. She cares deeply about people and ensures her company provides the highest level of customer satisfaction possible.

From day one, Sam has played a critical role on the front lines, perfecting the message and the company's overall image at every touchpoint. With every decision she is involved in, she considers the pros and cons from a reputation point of view.

Sam makes everyone feel like they've just met their new best friend. She connects with and inspires those she touches, naturally developing personal relationships with everyone she meets. People respond to her passion, integrity, and devotion to those around her.

Everyone sees Sam as the company's key representative, the figurehead, and the face of the operation. Every time she speaks, leads pour into the sales funnel. Her reputation is tied to the company's reputation, and she takes this very seriously.

Sam's startup success is highly dependent on her power to Connect. Her reputation convinces them that her company is unstoppable. Because of her industry stance, many early customers have jumped in with both feet, believing that anything Sam is involved with will be highly impactful.

As a result, everyone in the industry knows who Sam is and what her company does. Awareness is high, and she has people willing and ready to try her new product before it is ready for prime time.

Starting Point: Being Adept at Relationships

When Sam first started her company, many of her early customers were already her friends. They wanted to join her because they believed in her. Perhaps the product or services were still in the developmental stage, but Sam inspired them to trust and support her. As a result, these early adopters happily shared their experiences with other prospective customers, increasing the company's customer count early in the business's life.

As a Connector, Sam also connects on a personal level with her employees. While everyone knows Sam is in charge, she has an open-door policy, and people feel comfortable dropping by her office to ask questions or share ideas. Everyone at the company adores her. She has a way of inspiring employees around the mission, often attracting industry-relevant figures who want to work for the company.

The Two Key Descriptors

The two words that best describe a Connector are intuitive and people-oriented. They trust their gut, which is essential for relating to people. The Connector values compassion and cooperation and prefers collaboration to an authoritarian leadership style. Confrontation may not be their favorite thing, but they can stand their ground when needed. A Connector says, "My company helps people." Think Walt Disney.

Other Words that Describe the Connector Are:

motivational **connects**
relational **Caring** customer-obsessed
inquisitive **Humble** relational
Protects driven ideal reputable

Connectors Are Masters at "Owning Their Reputations"

Of the four Superpowers, Connectors are usually the most self-aware and self-referencing. They know who they are and what they want out of life and their new company. Connectors often see themselves as one of the startup's most significant assets. At first, the Connector and the company may seem to be synonymous, as they are based on the founder's personal and professional reputation.

That doesn't necessarily mean that Connectors are overly self-focused and egotistical. They are quite confident in what they bring to the industry and to their customers individually. Connectors instinctively know that the success of their startup is rooted in their own reputation and how they build on that reputation.

Consequently, they invest heavily in building strong, positive relationships among their customers and staff and within the industry. They are adept at networking, branding, customer satisfaction, and other elements that give their companies a leg up in the marketplace. I call this core competency "Own Your Reputation."

From day one, Connectors leverage their reputation to line up prospects to join the cause. As a result, they attract people willing to try something new, even if it is still being perfected. Like the Innovators, they appeal to early adopters who want to be on the ground floor. However, for Connectors, early buy-in has more to do with the buyer's relationship with the Connector than the product or service itself.

In order to Own Your Reputation, founders must have the perceptive skills to accurately assess how others feel and view them. These skills may not come naturally to the other three Superpowers, but the Connector reads people with ease. Connectors are very perceptive about others' feelings and opinions and can build bridges with many types of people. This trait empowers them to easily attract employees and customers who relate to their charisma and warm personalities.

Connectors intuitively know how to endear customers in a way that positively influences customers' feelings about the company. They start their company with industry involvement and rely initially on their reputation. Getting it right from the beginning is everything to them.

Another top priority is the company's culture. Connectors are hands-on and intentional about the culture they create in the workplace. The value they place on harmonious relationships helps them hire the right people. Culture isn't something that happens—they define it and, more importantly, live it with each action they take. Since employees are the most significant touchpoint with their customers, they hire for culture to guarantee their brand reputation remains stellar.

Given how much Connectors value how they and their companies are perceived, they strongly emphasize branding. While other Superpowers may put branding at the end of their to-do list, Connectors know that the secret to dominating the marketplace is how the company is presented to the public. A company's brand sets the tone with potential clients and colleagues in the industry. Consequently, Connectors' websites are usually well-designed, with carefully crafted written material and a highly stylized appearance.

Marketing efforts are rarely impersonal but communicate a strong emotional connection with potential customers. It means more organic growth, less reliance on paid advertising, more advocacy, and less churn. Every point of contact with the company is intentional to gain long-term buy-in, even before the product or service is ready for prime time. Connectors understand that how customers feel about the company is foundational to success.

Are You a Connector?

If you are a Connector, your business has been successful because you know how to create positive working relationships and involvement with the people around you. Your curiosity and passion are contagious. As a result, you naturally inspire teams to execute with extreme focus. Early employees follow you because they believe deeply in you as a person and a leader.

You are well-known in the industry you serve. Even if it is a new industry, you think outside the box and quickly get known for your charismatic personality. You have a way of "clicking" with people. As a result, you build personal relationships with influential people, including noteworthy prospects who become your first set of customers.

Your ability to Own Your Reputation also helps you attract top-notch talent to your company early on. These employees tend to be more seasoned and capable of helping bring your vision to life. They are willing to do what it takes because they sincerely believe in you and your cause.

Reflections:
- In what ways do you exhibit the traits of a Connector?
- What qualities of the Connector do you wish to develop?
- Are there elements of the Connector that feel completely foreign?

Side: A True Story of a Successful Connector

Guy Gal. That is a name that no one can forget. Between his unique name, provocative personality, and a gift of giving amazing hugs, Guy is a Connector through and through. How did it all start? Guy was talking to a friend of his who was a real estate agent at the time. His friend complained about how little support he got from his brokerage.

"Why don't you leave and go out on your own if it's that bad?" Guy asked him.

His friend responded that he wished he could. He said his clients don't care about which brokerage he is affiliated with. He explained that while he has made a name for himself, going out on his own would not only cost a lot of money but require a real estate agent to take on many risks since they would have to create their own brokerage. That was not something that his friend wanted to do. It was too operational and risky, so he decided to stay put.

Guy, on the other hand, took action. He was curious if other agents like his friend shared the same perception—that top agents don't need their brokerage's name or support and would disassociate with their brokerage if they could.

He spoke to dozens of top agents to confirm there was something to it. Guy forged relationships with many of the area's best, including Hilary Saunders, who ran her brokerage locally. In time, she became the chief brokerage officer at what eventually became Side—a service helping agents to own a boutique real estate company without the cost and risk of starting a new brokerage.

Guy had the dream and later brought on Ed Wu, an Innovator, who detailed what a white-label real estate brokerage platform would entail. Meanwhile, Guy continued to connect with local agents throughout Northern California, listening to their stories and inspiring them with the vision long before the product was ever ready to be launched. People made career-altering decisions based purely on Guy's dream and the deep relationship they had built with him.

———

Superpower #4:
The Power to Persuade
What will it take to get customers on board?

Meet Joe. Joe is just beginning his startup journey. He is so passionate about getting his product into his customers' hands that connecting with the end user exudes from every fiber of his being. Like Connectors, Persuaders are people-oriented. They are entertaining, rarely meet a stranger they don't like, and enjoy striking up conversations.

However, Joe is very mindful of his company's bottom line. In that regard, the Persuader and the Builder are similar. There's a point to Joe's relationship-building with customers and employees—to make his company successful financially. He knows he needs to relate well to people to achieve that goal. Whereas Builders drive numbers through process and data, Persuaders drive numbers through relationships and selling.

Starting Point: Being Confident and Convincing

Like most Persuaders, Joe is brimming with confidence, and he is certain that his company will succeed. After all, getting seed funding was easy, as was convincing some of his past colleagues to join the cause. He may only be partway through his first year of business, but he already has five customers engaged as he finishes out the first iteration of the product.

Joe's startup success is dependent on his Persuasion Superpower. Like Sam, he's a master storyteller who inspires people to believe they are unstoppable. He has a myriad of early wins based on the relationships he has built with his customers and feels great about the future ahead. His ability to gain buy-in from everyone he speaks with makes him feel invincible.

Everyone at Joe's startup wears multiple hats, including Joe as the founder and CEO. He is on the front line with potential customers. His ability to remember customer pain points and give examples from his first test customers is intoxicating. He builds trust by letting prospects into the tent regarding where the company is headed and getting them excited to be a participant. What the customer wants is what they get. Joe uses his power to Persuade customers and, with product and service teams companywide, ensures his customers are satisfied.

The Two Key Descriptors

The terms that best describe Persuaders are analytical and people-oriented. Think Tony Robbins. Persuaders are devoted to their company's success and achieve it by engaging with people to accomplish their goals.

Other Words that Describe the Persuader Are:

do-what-it-takes
storyteller **Inspirational**
calculated relational imaginative
Confident
Data-driven **charismatic**
motivational life of the party
proclivity for action

Persuaders Are Masters at "Winning Customers"

Persuaders focus on the bottom line: selling to customers. They know the sale is about providing obvious value to prospective customers, gaining trust, and convincing them to try their product or service. Persuaders are well-suited for this effort, which may seem obvious due to their storytelling and motivational skills. But it runs much deeper than that.

They express empathy and use customer stories and data points to speak with authority and conviction—three things required to ensure they can win them over. They have mastered the core competency and know how to Win Customers.

Being charismatic is the Persuader's secret weapon, but they don't build relationships with just anyone; they focus on key relationships that will help them move the business forward. They are data-driven and tend to retain important information about key relationships that would be useful later to seal the deal, whatever that deal is—joining the company, becoming a customer, negotiating a contract, etc. Persuaders do what it takes to get the job done. The Persuader will swoop in to save the day if the company is behind in revenue.

Are You a Persuader?

If you are a Persuader, your ability to win customers is the foundation of your success. You exude an overall likeability and negotiation prowess. It is easy for you to get people to buy into your vision, even those who initially didn't see the value. You love the thrill of the chase and strategize when people push back, finding new ways to motivate them into action.

Because you are so convincing, finding your first set of customers comes easy. But you may have to make a few promises to get them signed, which is par for the course. You have a lot of early success, leading the front-line sales efforts, which builds the team's overall confidence. People who work for you are in awe of your magician-like capabilities, often following your message as if it is gospel.

Your ability to persuade helps you hire great people because you can easily convince top talent to join the cause. You inspire teams and get them on the same page easily, which helps them rally around the same goals and objectives. You can get people fired up about whatever it is they need to tackle, giving them the feeling that they're ready to run into the fire.

You are also a master negotiator regarding cost-savings, which helps your company keep costs down while growing the top line. You see the world as one big negotiation and use your relatability and happy-go-lucky charm to drive results—and results are your focus, rain or shine.

Reflections:
- In what ways do you exhibit the traits of a Persuader?
- What qualities of the Persuader do you wish to develop?
- Are there elements of the Persuader that feel completely foreign?

Salesforce: A True Story of a Successful Persuader

In the last twenty years of my career, I have yet to work with a company that does not use Salesforce for its customer relationship management system (CRM). Why? No matter what you think of the tool itself, its ecosystem of applications that integrate with Salesforce makes it easy to do almost anything you are trying to accomplish for your business. (salesforceben.com, McCarthy, 2022)

So, how did Salesforce come about? It all started with a six-month sabbatical. Trailblazers, The Power of Business as the Greatest Platform for Change, Benioff, Marc Benioff was a former star salesman for Oracle, where he worked for thirteen years from 1986-1999. Here, he won rookie of the year at the age of twenty-three and eventually became their youngest vice president of all time. While at the top of his game, Marc felt he needed a break and took a six-month sabbatical to visit Hawaii and India. During this trip, he came up with the idea of Salesforce. He saw what companies like Amazon were doing online. He wondered why businesses were still loading and upgrading software when they could also do it online. (salesforceben.com, McCarthy, 2022)

So how did this former sales professional, who sold software at the age of fifteen and eventually earned enough to pay his way through college, start the cloud-based software as a service (SaaS) phenomenon? He found three incredible software developers to build out his vision in a tiny one bedroom apartment on Telegraph Hill—Parker Harris, Frank Dominguez, and Dave Moellenhoff.

By the end of their first year together, they had forty employees and were ready for the official launch. That was where Marc's storytelling skills came into play. According to Salesforceben.com, the Salesforce launch event occurred at the San Francisco Regency Theater, and fifteen hundred people were in attendance. They turned the theater's lower level into "Enterprise Software Hell" with screaming sales-people in cages and games such as whack-a-mole, where the moles were other software companies. Once attendees made it through this experience, they were escorted upstairs to experience "Salesforce. com." Alongside this launch event, Marc and his team rolled out what would become a tagline synonymous with Salesforce—"No Software." They also had an ad campaign launch with fighter jets shooting down a biplane, representing the software industry becoming obsolete.

In 2003 the first Dreamforce conference was born, which would eventually grow to tens of thousands of attendees each year. At Dreamforce, Marc could take the stage and update sales, marketing, and developers from around the world on new product launches all in one place. By 2008, Forbes named Salesforce the fastest growing technology company in the world, helping to skyrocket their userbase to over fifty five thousand users. (thestreet. com, Salvucci, 2024)

Fast-forward to today, and Marc Benioff is still the CEO at Salesforce with dozens of acquisitions under his belt. The company is now worth close to two hundred and eighty billion dollars, and Marc himself has a net worth just shy of ten billion dollars.

———

Part I: Summary Chart

Founder	Innovator (NT)	Builder (ST)	Connector (NF)	Persuader (SF)
Key Descriptors	Intuitive and Logical	Analytical and Logical	Intuitive and people-oriented	Analytic and people-oriented
G-R-O-W Competency	Gain Conviction	Ramp Up	Own Your Reputation	Win Customers
Strengths	Curious and Creative Optimistic and Future-oriented Able to tolerate high-risk	Creates and follows plans Analytical, and data-driven Action-oriented	Prioritizes relationships Fosters a positive work culture Influential in the industry	Confident and convincing Pragmatic and Action-oriented Motivated to succeed

PART II

WHY IS YOUR STARTUP NOW STRUGGLING TO SCALE?

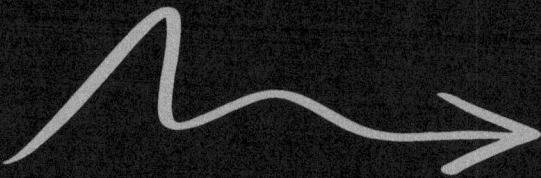

CHAPTER 3

The Four Competencies Required to G-R-O-W

"Success is simply a matter of finding and surrounding ourselves with those open-minded and clever souls who can take our insanity and put it to good use."
–Anita Roddick, founder of The Body Shop

Congratulations! You now know more about your Superpower and that a company can be successfully launched when the founder relies on the core competency of one primary Superpower. You know this firsthand since your Superpower has already garnered a good deal of success in the first weeks, months, or years you have been in business. Your startup mindset served you well during the initial stage of launching your company.

In contrast, a GrowUp mindset recognizes what ninety percent of founders fail to see: To be successful, you can't rely on your Superpower alone. For a business to truly GrowUp, the core competencies of all four Superpowers must be in play.

It Takes All Four Competencies to GrowUp!

Imagine that you're building a house on a square foundation. At each corner of the building, you'll need a cornerstone. If the builder tries to lay a floor on a single stone, it won't be sturdy enough to build an entire structure. With two cornerstones, the house would teeter to one side or the other. It's rather apparent where I'm going with this. A house needs all four corners to lay a strong foundation and construct a building that will stand the test of time.

An organization is similar. Four corners are needed, each supplied by a different Superpower necessary to scale. Without all four G-R-O-W competencies, portions of your organization are likely underdeveloped or missing altogether.

All four core competencies are needed to GrowUp. The Innovator develops a product that meets a felt-need for customers and knows how to Gain Conviction. The Builder's skills are needed for operations, management, and keeping money coming in and the doors open so that the company can Ramp Up. The Connector's strengths secure a place in your chosen industry with a clear brand, online presence, and market position so that you can Own Your Reputation. Persuaders drive your sales efforts to Win Customers. They have a pulse on what customers are buying and how your company stacks up to the competition and gets the product sold. One core competency alone won't do the job.

And yet, most entrepreneurs rely primarily, if not solely, on what they do best—*their* Superpower—the personality traits that fuel

their business core competency. Even if they have hired people for these roles, the Superpowers those people hold may not be diverse enough to master all of the core competencies necessary. Entrepreneurs who go through the trouble of starting new businesses, with the odds for survival as bad as they are, must firmly believe in themselves and their product, process, brand, and sales potential. But all too often, startups are led by people who overestimate their power and overlook the need for the other three Superpowers.

> **"**
>
> Your company has one-fourth of what is needed to succeed. And this is why so many startups never GrowUp.

I am not minimizing what you bring to the table or trying to diminish your achievements in any way. What you have done is nothing short of remarkable. The challenge is to see that your company has one-fourth of what is needed to succeed. And this is why so many startups never GrowUp.

In the next section, we will explore in more depth how you can move your business from a startup mindset to a GrowUp perspective by including the core competencies of each Superpower. You can see that while you may have relied heavily on your strengths, the future will be won or lost on how well you've put all four core competencies into action.

The Four G-R-O-W Competencies:

G: Gain Conviction – The Innovator
R: Ramp Up – The Builder
O: Own Your Reputation – The Connector
W: Win Customers – The Persuader

Gain Conviction: A company led by an Innovator has a viable product or service that their target audience wants to buy. But how will customers find what they need if that company isn't well-funded or has no marketplace presence?

Ramp Up: If you're a Builder, you may have all the processes and reporting in place, and investors may be waiting to hand over money. But what happens if your company isn't well known and your product isn't differentiated?

Own Your Reputation: As a Connector, you probably know all of the influencers in your industry and have a compelling story behind your company. Everyone knows how to find you, but what if the product delivery process has been neglected or there is no call to action so sales can occur?

Win Customers: You may be amazing at closing deals, but retention will be difficult if your product or service doesn't meet your customers' needs once they use it. Without product-market fit, will you have a strong presence in the marketplace or a growing pipeline of prospects?

GROW

G AIN CONVICTION

R AMP UP

O WN YOUR REPUTATION

W IN CUSTOMERS

CHAPTER 4

Gain Conviction:
The Superpower of Innovation

*"Don't find customers for your products,
find products for your customers."*
—Seth Godin

You've met Jane the Innovator, who conceived a way to automate the sales process for small to mid-sized companies. In her previous role as a business consultant, she'd had the opportunity to observe dozens of sales teams struggling to become more efficient while using conventional sales methods. Since Innovators often think "outside the box," Jane looked at the problem from a new perspective and came up with a fresh idea to solve the issue.

Before anyone programmed a single bit of code to implement her idea, Jane interviewed most of her ex-clients to understand their pain points. She shadowed their day-to-day operation and uncovered all the problems they had across the entire sales cycle.

But she didn't stop there. She asked each of them for introductions to additional sales professionals to expand her reach. Jane spoke to companies big and small. Patterns emerged among the frustrations, especially for sales teams with thirty or fewer sales-people. Regardless of the company in which they worked, these smaller sales teams complained about doing time-consuming administrative tasks that took them away from reaching out to prospects. She discovered this problem was less prevalent for larger companies with the resources to bring on support staff and a myriad of complex tooling they could throw at the problem. From these interviews, Jane knew she was on to something—if she could help these smaller teams be more efficient without breaking the bank, she would have a winning product.

Her next step was to see if enough companies fit her param-eters. She identified millions of such companies she could help in the U.S. alone. She asked herself how to deliver an affordable tool that automates the sales process for this under-resourced customer segment.

Jane got to work. She reached out to a good friend, an extreme-ly talented software engineer, and convinced him to be her partner in crime. Sitting around Jane's kitchen table, they took inventory of all the administrative tasks these teams were doing per Jane's research. They bucketed them into things that were easy versus difficult to automate. Given the limited budgets of these small to midsized companies, they knew they couldn't add a lot of bells and whistles that would incur significant data integration costs. They would need to keep the product lightweight and go for solving the low-hanging fruit problems without a lot of overhead.

Keeping it simple was challenging for Jane's software engineer-ing co-founder, who was drawn to solving complex problems. But Jane kept pulling him back to refocus. She knew that if they made it too complicated, the product would not be accessible to the cus-tomer segment that needed it most.

Once a prototype was ready, Jane and her co-founder selected a few teams they knew to pilot the product. The first iteration was clunky, but they were able to iterate quickly with feedback streaming in from day-to-day users. After evolving the product with user feedback for almost a year, Jane and her co-founder were ready to spread their wings. Their pilot customers reported significant efficiency gains, numbers they could confidently quote when approaching new customers. By the middle of their second year, they had more than a dozen paying customers and were ready to add more people to the team to expedite their growth.

With paying customers committed, Jane *gained the conviction* necessary to build out her company. She knew she had a solution to a widely held felt need and a means to deliver that solution. That is called product-market fit.

"Product-Market Fit"

Product-market fit describes a scenario in which a company's target customers are buying, using, and telling others about the company's product in numbers large enough to sustain that product's growth and profitability. (productplan.com/glossary)

Has Your Company Gained Conviction?

Now let's look at your company. Has your business gained conviction around product-market fit?

The first step is confirming that you have clearly identified a specific problem or a collection of problems that are a pain point for potential customers. Do you comprehensively understand all the friction points your customers face? That isn't achieved simply by having an idea them in your mind. Rather, you need to talk to as many potential customers as possible and observe their day-to-day lives. There may be pain points that people aren't even aware of, but they could be meaningful to tackle.

Furthermore, creating a product or service that meets the identified need(s) is essential. Have you engaged in the research needed to verify the viability of your product? What articles have you read? Who have you talked with about your proposed solution? Potential customers? Others in the industry? Your employees or consultants?

Putting oneself in the customers' shoes allows a company to understand which of their clients their ideas will resonate with most. You may need to increase your comfort and skill level at engaging in these conversations and narrow down the type of individual to start with—their demographics, interests, and behaviors are all part of the equation.

After you've identified a felt need and proposed a product to meet that need, the next step is validating the size of your potential customer base. Are enough people willing to pay for the solution to make your efforts worthwhile?

Companies that have *Gained Conviction* know that to build a viable business, they need confidence that their solution has broad appeal. So, once they know who will buy their product out of the gate, the Innovator researches to identify the number of people who loosely match that initial customer profile in the locations they are targeting. This number is called the "Total Addressable Market" (TAM)—the total population of people who may be interested in buying a particular product.

As you talk with potential customers, be careful not to fall into the trap of customers telling you what they want your solution to look like. If Henry Ford listened to what his customers said they wanted, he would have built a faster horse instead of a car. Innovators understand this well. If the customer is describing a solution, they thank the customer and pivot the conversation back to the problem at hand. They don't set false expectations around what they will or won't do to fix those problems. They intuitively know that if they let customer ideas creep in, the company will end up with an endless list of enhancements that will never suffice.

A great example of finding a unique solution to a problem is the Nintendo Wii. Suppose Nintendo had gone out to gamers and asked what would make a better gaming console. In that case, they may have heard about a desire for better graphics, better speed, and other reactions to the current gaming devices on the market. But Nintendo didn't want to be like the other gaming devices. The goal was to try to appeal to a much broader audience. So, what did Nintendo do? They conducted market research with a broader group of customers, including moms, to develop new thinking around gaming.

Here are some problems identified by interviewing moms: Moms said that current machines were difficult to use, complicated to start, drained energy, and were loud while running. "Rather than just picking new technology, we thought seriously about what a game console should be. [CEO Satoru] wanted a console that would play every Nintendo game ever made. Moms would hate it if they had to have several consoles lying around." – *Shigeru Miyamoto, Nintendo Wii video game designer* (money.yahoo.com, Businessweek Interviews Miyamoto and Ashida About the Wii, Hinkle, 2006-11-16)

As you can see from this Nintendo example, the company identified crucial problems in these interviews, understood the mindset of these moms, and came up with a unique solution. That should always be the goal of interviews, not to learn what they want but to learn what their problems are. If you fall into the trap of customers telling you what they want, thank them and pivot the conversation. Ask them what problems they think those ideas will solve. Don't set false expectations around what you will or won't do to fix those problems. If you don't do this, you will end up with an endless list of enhancements that will never suffice.

What Happens to a Company that Has Not Gained Conviction?

Thirty percent of startups fail because there is no market need. Even when you have a healthy number of paying customers who are very satisfied with the product or service, it is possible that you don't have enough product-market fit to sustain that growth over time. Product-market fit needs to be continuously validated as you grow. If you don't have an Innovator, reaching the GrowUp status you desperately seek will be impossible. (cbinsights.com, The Top Twelve Reasons Startups Fail, 2021)

To be clear, I am not saying that only Innovators try to solve problems. However, Innovators are uniquely equipped to understand product-market fit. If you do not have an Innovator in your company, it becomes more about the depths you must go to validate a problem. In my experience, Builders, Connectors, and Persuaders, build solutions to problems they or someone they are closed to have experienced. They don't go deep enough to ensure a sustainable market for their products and services.

If you are not an Innovator, it seems obvious that *everyone like you* experiences the problem you have encountered. Your initial customer base likely validated this. The company was born and you started ramping up. You think to yourself, "My initial customers love what we do. Therefore, everyone will." *That does not meet the standards of gaining conviction.*

Innovators require more input from customers than the other three Superpowers, who can fall prey to what I call the "shiny puppy syndrome"— having a product that everyone says they want but is unwilling to pay for. Everyone says they want a solution to a problem, but when it comes to product market-fit, the rubber meets the road when money changes hands.

> " Everyone says they want a solution to a problem, but when it comes to product-market fit, the rubber meets the road when money changes hands.

Years ago, I worked with a purpose-driven startup selling technology to Fortune 500 companies across the country. It was a great idea on the surface, and I was brought into the mission almost immediately. A few clients had beta-tested the platform but had yet to sign any of these Fortune 500 companies up as paying customers. (fortune.com/ranking/fortune500/)

When I asked the head of sales about it, he would always tell me how promising it was and that no one had yet said no. To him, it all felt like part of a long sales cycle in warming the doorknobs enough to get the yes he was seeking. I believed it was a red flag that no one had said no. It meant we weren't sure why clients were rejecting the platform.

See, the thing about selling a world-impacting mission is that it *feels* good. It is like the puppy in the window at the pet store. The puppy is absolutely adorable, so I ogle it every time I walk by. I may even go in and pet it. But when it comes to pulling out my pocketbook to adopt the puppy, I stop myself. Why? Because I don't need that puppy right now. As cute as it is, I have a dog at home, and a new puppy might complicate my lifestyle and not be conducive to all the traveling I want to do. The purpose-driven startup suffered from the shiny puppy syndrome. Everyone drooled over it, but very few people were willing to buy it, proving that the product-market fit was not strong enough for it to penetrate the marketplace with its existing solution.

This startup needed to dig deeper and uncover meaningful problems that people are willing to spend money fixing. As a result, the existing team missed the mark, making several mistakes in the early days of their company's journey. It is important to recognize that each Superpower tends to make unique mistakes as it relates to the other three core competencies. Let's spend a few minutes reviewing the mistakes each Superpower could fall prey to if they do not have an Innovator leading the way.

A Builder's Mistake:
Believing that Data Is All You Need

You met Rich, the Builder, in chapter one. Rich grew his company's revenue steadily year after year. He implemented all the processes and procedures needed to scale the business effectively as his revenue grew.

Because Rich's nature is analytical, he spotted a market trend and built a product similar to an existing one. After all, his data showed that there was enough market share to go around. And for the first three years, there was. Rich and his operationally savvy team brought on hundreds of customers, perfecting the sales and support process along the way.

Rich was proud of the predictability of their sales process. For every one hundred leads, he knew that twenty percent would show purchase intent and fifty percent of those would buy. Their confidence was so high that they upped their marketing spend to increase volume. That initially led to more sales—until it didn't.

Rich and his team were scratching their heads. Were they suddenly getting bad leads into the sales funnel? They dove deep into a sampling of leads, but the characteristics of these prospects were the same as those before.

As Rich's leadership team soon pointed out, new sales were down, and the company's churn rate was also increasing. They were losing current customers faster than they were acquiring new ones!

Rich turned to his marketing lead to do a deep dive into the competition. He found that his initial competitor had added new product features that were drawing customers away. But even more impactful was discovering a brand-new competitor recently hit the scene with a modern user interface and a lot more bells and whistles than he had.

Both companies were taking Rich's market share. He was behind the curve and with revenue forecasts down for the first time since the company's inception, Rich needed to let some people go while he figured out how to catch up from a feature perspective.

If Rich had an Innovator on his leadership team, the company's target audience's problems would have been the team's ongoing focus. They would have launched with a better product than the leading competitor, solving issues that the competitor did not, and they would have kept their eye on the ball to keep their competitive edge.

A Connector's Mistake:
Believing You Are the Product

You also met Sam the Connector in the third year of her startup journey. She spent most of her time building relationships with her startup team, customers, and others in the industry she serves.

Sam's company was built around the buzzword of the year—AI. It was a hot topic at all the industry events, and everyone was trying to figure out how this new capability could create industry-wide value. Since Sam knew the industry well, she had a good handle on different ways artificial intelligence could, in theory, impact the industry, so she started waxing poetic about what might be possible.

She said, "Imagine a world where this long, arduous task was something you could do in under five minutes." Given her reputation, people were enamored with her pontifications. They encouraged Sam to start a company that could do all the things she mentioned. Many of the people who joined her team early on were the very people who had encouraged her from the onset.

Three years later, Sam had started an AI solution, and she had accumulated a fairly sizable team who wanted to be alongside her on the ground floor of disruption. As promised, they had figured out how to take a task that typically took hours to complete and reduce it to just a few minutes.

Sam's startup success was built on her reputation. Because of her industry stance, many early customers initially jumped in with both feet, believing that anything Sam was involved with would be highly impactful. She continued to speak on the topic at industry conferences, and new customers would come pouring in the door every time she did.

However, customer usage dwindled within thirty days of signing up for Sam's product. Even though the software had sped up an important task, Sam and her team missed a regulatory requirement that had to occur outside of her system's control. Something they would have known if they had gone much deeper into the end to end process used by their customer set.

Even her friends in the industry who knew the process didn't put two and two together, as their teams, not them, did the work that Sam's company was automating. By the third or fourth month, usage was pretty non-existent. Given Sam's relationship with each customer, they rarely canceled, but they weren't using the product. They provided references as a personal favor to Sam, but that was it. As the company expanded beyond Sam's immediate connections, churn grew extensively, losing customers faster than it gained them.

When Sam started to hear chatter in the industry about her product, she took it very seriously. After all, her reputation was at stake. Even some of her initial customers, her most prominent advocates, started to cancel. Sam huddled with her team to determine where they went wrong.

If Sam had an Innovator on her team, they would have known from the get-go that the task they were trying to automate took the same amount of time with or without the AI because of regulatory checks and balances that needed to occur. It had nothing to do with the time it took internal teams but the wait time required to get approvals. An Innovator wouldn't have started with the solution of AI; they would have started by deeply understanding the problem at hand.

A Persuader's Mistake:
Believing a Good Pitch Can Compensate
for Product-Market Fit

Joe, the Persuader is the founder at the beginning of his startup journey. His company was built around a problem that he had experienced firsthand. His personal story was so compelling, and he told it with such confidence that he easily convinced investors to provide seed funding and employees to join the company.

Potential customers were drawn to Joe as well. Before the team had completed the product's first iteration, he had already signed up five paying customers. Joe was great with numbers, and since his first customers were just like him, he used their success stories to convince additional customers to try his product.

Joe and his team had the pitch down pat, and as more customers signed up, Joe began to feel invincible. A decent percentage of his network was now using the product regularly. Like Rich, the Builder, Joe had no problem building a sales machine. Within the first few months, they signed up customers faster than they could onboard them.

However, once they bridged outside of Joe's network, things started to slow down, and Joe couldn't figure out why. No other companies were doing what they were doing in the marketplace, so why weren't they continuing to make a splash? Their pitch remained strong with lots of interest, but the percentage of customers signing contracts stopped, with many prospects telling them to check in later. Without a definitive no, Joe and his team were left very confused especially since they had a bunch of paying customers that were quite happy. Where was the word of mouth? Why wasn't their customer success sealing the deal with others?

If Joe had an Innovator on his team, he would have known that the population of people like him was small. He had assumed that a problem he was addressing was also a big problem for everyone else. But that assumption was not accurate. Joe and his team failed to talk to potential customers beyond his own experience and then do the proper research to size the market before they started the company.

In Joe's case, he was solving a very niche-use issue. While it was attractive to other people, the problem wasn't big enough for them to pay to solve it with any kind of urgency. In the end, Joe and his team had the shiny puppy syndrome. People thought the idea was noble and liked the concept, but the problem wasn't big enough to pay to solve.

Reflections:
- Does someone in your company have the Superpower of Innovation?
- Do any of the mistakes made by other Superpowers resonate with you?

On a scale from 1 to 10, rate the degree to which your company has Gained Conviction. Does your company have product-market fit?

1-2	No, we're in trouble
3-5	Some, needs attention
6-8	Good, could improve
9-10	Great, it's the best thing we do!

1	2	3	4	5	6	7	8	9	10

CHAPTER 5

Ramp Up:
The Superpower of Building

"What gets measured gets improved."
—Peter Drucker

Rich the Builder spotted a trend in the market and brought a product to bear at the right time to compete with more established companies. His company's revenue grew steadily year over year because he had put processes and procedures in place to scale the business effectively.

For Rich, this was the plan from the beginning. From day one, Rich started documenting everything he would need to implement to turn his idea into a successful business. This detailed plan gave Rich the confidence to proceed. He outlined all the startup costs in detail, including the people he would need in place both from the beginning and as the company grew.

But he didn't stop there. The plan spelled out his growth strategy, all the materials he would need, the crucial partnerships he would create, his revenue objectives, and the key performance indicators that would have to be met to invest more in the company as time went on. He had the first several years of financials spelled out, including a comprehensive fundraising plan.

Having a solid business plan enabled Rich to get initial seed funding from former colleagues and family members, but hitting his goals in the first few years is what secured a more significant investment by a well-known venture capital firm in year three.

Rich thrived on data and setting up a predictable process that guaranteed his success. His love for graphs and charts highlighting the strength of his results is what won over investors and potential employees alike. He hired people with decades of operational experience to set up and run each department. These seasoned leaders created specific processes and held their teams accountable for hitting the plan. As a result, there were very few surprises along the way.

When Rich noticed that customer retention had dipped a tad on the executive dashboard, he made no assumptions as to why. Instead, his team got to work, investigating dozens of other data points to uncover the root cause. It turned out that their customer service levels had also dipped a few basis points. To solve the problem, Rich's head of customer support hired two more customer support representatives a few months ahead of the plan to handle the incremental volume.

Now in his fifth year of business, Rich has successfully ramped up to full capacity based on his initial business plan. The company has shown a steady ten percent year over year growth rate, and Rich enjoys the predictability of it all. He has built a well-oiled machine. As a result, he can take a well-deserved vacation, recognizing that he has the right team in place to address any issues that arise with or without him there.

Has Your Company Ramped Up?

Now let's examine your company. A founder of a company that is able to Ramp Up has well-structured documents that outline goals, financial viability, policies and procedures, and, quite often, a clear exit strategy before the door even opens. If you're not a Builder, these might not be as developed as required, or may not exist at all.

Companies that successfully Ramp Up love being prepared. Nothing can get them more prepared than thinking through all the elements of a business plan, including different scenarios of what might happen over time. Do you have a way of collecting relevant data so that facts, not just opinions or intuition, are involved in decision-making? Do you know the size of the market, your competitor's market share, market pricing, development costs, acquisition costs, and so forth? Have you thought through multiple scenarios and modeled them out on paper?

Why do companies that have successfully Ramped Up create business plans? Because having a framework in which to operate the company and test assumptions is the only thing that provides the confidence necessary to invest time and money on the company itself. A company prepared to Ramp Up has a way to gather and analyze all of the data and then model it out. *This is not a one-and-done initiative.* At every step of growth, it's critical to gather new information because as your business grows, the problems you face will change. Your model will need to be continually tweaked and revised. So, as the company scales, successful founders keep their eye on the ball as it relates to inputs, making sure the company is growing at the right pace and using resources effectively to be sustainable over time.

Once your company has put a business plan in place, it's time to turn your attention to processes, procedures, and key performance indicators (KPIs) so you can gauge how the company is performing according to the plan. These define the nuts and bolts of how the company will be run. This step includes creating organizational charts, job descriptions, hiring procedures, detailed processes, and defining all of the specific and measurable goals and objectives.

Successful leaders see personnel and other expenses as necessary inputs to accomplish their planned outputs. They detail how they will build and deliver their offering and then project out what they will need to put in place to make that happen over time using carefully thought-out assumptions. As a result, they tend to have a financially viable, well-organized group of people who build and deliver their products and services with clearly defined roles and expectations.

Companies Ramp Up successfully because they rely on hard facts and, as a result, will identify all of the KPIs necessary to track the business's health. It is not just revenue and cost metrics; those are outcomes of the inputs, but the key metrics that can predict those outcomes along the way. Things like sales pipeline, customer growth, customer acquisition costs, customer satisfaction, customer retention, employee engagement, etc., are all common KPIs that a Builder will figure out how to measure early on. How does your company demonstrate these needed goals?

One of the most helpful aspects of the Builder's core competency is being able to predict outcomes. That might be an obvious statement, but planning for a successful future is essential to survival. Are you involved in developing and optimizing processes to derive at your desired outcome

> **Planning for a successful future is essential to survival.**

each and every time? Do you have written organizational charts and clear job descriptions so that everyone knows their roles and how to be personally successful?

This investment in process and order is essential to companies that Ramp Up successfully, especially when it comes to showing investors and stakeholders that this company can stand the test of time. It builds confidence in financial projections, and ultimately, makes raising money easier if they need it.

You might not be a natural at these tasks, but it will undoubtedly pay off when you can wow investors with past performance and growth projections. Once you've analyzed all the business data to the nth degree, you can feel highly confident dealing with whatever is thrown your way. You can take center stage in larger fundraising rounds. If an investor asks for more data, you will be more than up for the challenge. With a solid business plan in place and all the metrics you are tracking across the company, you will have what it takes to turn the most uncertain investor into a believer of the company's potential.

What Happens to a Company That Can't Ramp Up?

Have you ever heard of a company called Munchery? Munchery was one of the very first companies to offer meal delivery as a service. When it opened its doors in 2010, it hired a bunch of gourmet chefs to create uniquely crafted and continually changing menu items that consumers could order and have delivered directly to their doorsteps. While many services like this exist today, such as Blue Apron, HelloFresh, Home Chef, etc., Munchery was among the first to hit the scene before closing its doors in 2019.

Munchery's demise initially had nothing to do with funding. Munchery had raised over $125 million across eight different fundraising events, had one hundred-plus employees, and was valued at $300+ million. They prided themselves on the convenience of their service, the quality control they offered by having their own chefs, and their undying focus on optimizing the efficiency of their couriers. (techcrunch.com/2019/01/21/munchery-shuts-down/, Clark)

What went wrong at Munchery? According to the new Munchery.com "About" page, the meal kit service faced increasing costs to produce and deliver their meals at the right level of quality in a way that enabled the company to be profitable. Their promise of quality had geographical constraints since they would have to deliver food within a short drive of the kitchen. To compensate, they rapidly expanded their footprint, setting up kitchens in major cities nationwide. That became very costly. New competitors hit the scene in the form of restaurant delivery platforms such as Uber Eats and DoorDash, and these were far more cost-efficient to operate since they were leveraging local restaurants. While having chefs on staff was once their key differentiator to control quality, it eventually became Munchery's Achilles heel. With rising costs and increased market competition, Munchery was unable to raise additional financing and was forced to shut down its meal kit service in January 2019, much to the disappointment of its customers.

How could Munchery have managed its business differently? After all, in the beginning, they appeared to have a great product-market fit and enough customers willing to pay for their service. Revenue was good—so good that investors continued to invest in their growth time and time again. Doing what it takes initially makes sense, but you must anticipate and plan for the future. Munchery didn't have a thoroughly thought-out plan to scale locations cost-effectively.

If your company has yet to Ramp Up successfully, then chances are setting goals and, more importantly, tracking your progress is not your jam. You will be caught off guard when things don't work out as expected. That will not only impact your ability to scale in the long term but will have short-term implications as well.

Hopefully, someone on your team is a Builder, but if not, having someone who plants their flag square within this Superpower will be vital for your continued effective business management. But they don't have to be full-time if you can't afford to do so right away. Find a mentor who is a Builder or consultant who can help you get these capabilities off the ground as early as possible.

Why? Because when it comes to goal setting, you need to ask yourself the hard questions. For instance, if you have a revenue goal to get to $100,000 per month, what will that take? How many customers do you need to acquire and at what price point? How are you going to know if you will have enough customers? Do you have enough prospects? How many do you need? How are you going to get those prospects? Do you need more salespeople? Do you need more marketing? How are you going to retain these customers? What retention rate are you assuming in your plan? How are you going to know if retention starts to wane? What early signals can you track? Is it customer service tickets? Feature requests?

If you dig in, ask many questions, and sift through the layers as part of your business plan, you will be able to react and make adjustments quickly. If you think about it, having a plan is the most startup thing you can do, as it allows you to be nimble and adjust speedily.

With goals and KPIs to assess results, you can predict revenue and cost needs to raise money, ramp the company up, let alone keep the company afloat.

That is precisely what happened to Munchery. If Munchery had brought a

> **"**
> Having a plan is the most startup thing you can do.

robust Builder into the mix, they would have analyzed all of the ways they could scale efficiently and would have pivoted to survive. Instead, what once was an incredible company full of Innovators, solving real problems, had to close their doors. Not having the proper core competencies in place to Ramp Up cost Munchery their business, which is a scary thing to contemplate for any start-up. Let's take a look at the mistakes these Innovators likely made without a Builder to help them plan and execute, alongside the other two Superpowers and their potential for mistakes when a Builder is missing from the equation.

An Innovator's Mistake:
Believing Speed Matters Most

Jane, the Innovator who built technology to automate process for small to mid-sized sales teams, hated the word "process" inside her own company. To Jane, process is where innovation goes to die because it significantly slows down teams and what they are able to bring to market. In her eyes, it removes the ability for teams to be nimble and adjust quickly when the market demands it. She has a great story from the first six months of her startup to prove it.

When Jane first launched in the market, her software was only built for sales leadership to administer automation globally. Still, when Jane visited a few of their initial customers, she discovered that many salespeople were circumventing the system because they couldn't customize anything happening. In essence, the very people the technology was built to make more efficient were not using the product at all. With this insight in mind, Jane quickly brought her small but exceptionally talented product and engineering team together and did a two-week sprint that built flexibility into the system for the sales professionals themselves. They rolled it out in a limited beta and increased overall utilization of their system by thirty-five percent in less than one month. After that, the team built more and more functionality into the application for the sales professionals themselves, in essence expanding the reach of their product offering in ways that had salespeople who had experienced the tool at one company recommending it at another. This simple pivot doubled the company's revenue in less than six months.

However, as more customers were onboarding, more feature requests and system issues were reported. Now the same number of product managers and engineers needed to balance significant new features with small requests and bug fixes. Since there was no process in place to prioritize these requests, very few customer requests got handled. Instead, the team led by Innovator Jane kept tackling big rock items that would move the product forward in a material way.

When one of the product managers suggested hiring more engineers to handle both big rock projects and customers' requests, Jane blew up at him. In her mind, adding resources would mean adding layers of management that would slow them down, not speed them up. She thought they would have more people producing the same amount of work.

Over time, while customers were wowed by new features, they were frustrated with the platform's little idiosyncrasies, which made it difficult for them to accomplish some of the more basic tasks. Small requests like the ability to copy and customize a template were lost in the shuffle.

If Jane had a solid Builder by her side, there would have been a standard process to prioritize requests, giving Jane a sense of everything that needed to be accomplished simultaneously. A trusted Builder would have worked with Jane on a plan to get her comfortable adding resources without slowing their output down.

A Connector's Mistake:
Believing They Are the Key Decision-Maker

Sam the Connector built her company on top of *her* reputation. As a result, she felt that every action the company took within the industry directly impacted people's perception of her. Sam learned this the hard way early on when an email went out to current customers from customer support that rubbed everyone the wrong way. Given Sam's deep relationships with her early customers, she was inundated with calls from customers upset by the sudden change communicated—something completely avoidable if more context was given.

Sam's solution ran counter to setting her company up for growth. Instead of properly training her customer services team, Sam made it her business to review every communication sent to customers or prospects. She reviewed every word in minute detail, making edits to ensure everything was on point. Over time, this review extended to any decision that could impact customers, good or bad. Nothing could move forward without her blessing.

This review process was okay in the beginning. Then, as the company grew, so many decisions had to be made that having Sam involved became a significant bottleneck. As she tried to juggle industry appearances with meetings to make fundamental decisions, the team's ability to move things forward came to a crawl. If she were unavailable, critical decisions would wait weeks, if not months.

With substantial delays in the company's decision-making, business slowed down markedly. Competitors gained traction, and Sam's company lost market share.

If Sam had a Builder on her team, the Builder would have pointed out this process challenge. They would have documented the decision criteria and created a framework for Sam to approve for future use. That would have put Sam's mind at ease, knowing that her decision-making framework and messaging preferences would be followed consistently. Instead of getting burnt out trying to maintain relationships while having her hands on everything happening at the company, she would have been able to focus on what she does best—connecting with people and sharing the company vision across the industry at large.

A Persuader's Mistake: Believing Anything is Possible

Jim the Persuader, who brought on customers long before their product was ready to go to market, had the gift of the gab. It only took a few months before Jim perfected the pitch using data and customer stories to persuade prospects to do business with them. By the end of year one, he had already built a well-oiled sales machine that could sign up customers faster than the company could onboard them.

Jim was a great source of enhancement requests as the product evolved. The head of product development called him frequently to understand what the product lacked. If there were a feature that the product didn't have, Jim would tell the prospect that the feature was in the works. After all, given his relationship with product the lead, it often was. Whenever Jim found a feature that would close a new deal, he convinced the product lead to add the enhancement to the queue, making the development team scramble to execute against all of his one-off requests.

The team was so reactionary to new prospect requests that big enhancements that could help all customers get much more value from the product were wildly delayed—some never seeing the light of day. Even worse, with dozens of custom features implemented for specific customers, the core platform was impossible to update without excessive QA against all the made-to-order features to ensure they were still operational. By the time Jim was in year five, many of his initial customers were still on the product's first version. Without all the value adds necessary to keep the product relevant, these initial customers began to cancel.

This would not have happened if there had been a Builder on the leadership team. The Builder would have carefully planned out and executed the value-added enhancements needed to advance the product, keeping churn rates low. There would have been a process to assess new prospect requests to ensure they would benefit the masses before putting them on the roadmap. If they were deemed valuable, another process would have been in place to evaluate the feature request's value over other enhancements in the queue.

Reflections:

- Does someone in your company have the Superpower to Build?
- Do any of the mistakes made by other Superpowers resonate with you?

On a scale from 1 to 10, rate the degree to which your company has Ramped Up.

1-2	No, we're in trouble
3-5	Some, needs attention
6-8	Good, could improve
9-10	Great, it's the best thing we do!

1	2	3	4	5	6	7	8	9	10

CHAPTER 6

Own Your Reputation: The Superpower of Connection

"It takes twenty years to build a reputation and five minutes to ruin it." –Warren Buffett

Sam the Connector has a long history within the industry she serves. She has held positions at some of the most prestigious companies and, as a result, broke into the speaking circuit early on, waxing poetic about ways to improve the customer experience. Her ability to deliver compelling speeches was unmatched by most. Her sessions were often packed to the rim, inspiring people to take action.

Sam was so plugged in with other thought leaders across the industry that she always knew the hot topics people were mulling over. While she wasn't originally an AI expert, her industry connections began discussing the topic at length and building hypotheses around what it could do to make the industry more efficient, so Sam followed suit. She started to pontificate on what was possible, and as a result, people listened. So much so that key people in the industry encouraged Sam to start a company that does everything she spoke about.

Over the next year, Sam hired a development team and had the start of an AI solution in place. She brought in several people from her network to help build out the company. Everyone wanted to be on the ground floor with Sam because they believed in her greatness as a thought leader.

Before the company officially launched its first product for sale, Sam had dozens of customers lining up to be first to market with her solution. Her position in the industry put the company on the map. Awareness was high. Everyone was waiting with bated breath to experience what she had built for the first time.

When they finally launched the product, Sam made sure the positioning was on point. After all, she had been talking about the capabilities for months now, so it was natural for Sam to translate her thought leadership into product messaging on their company website and throughout all of their sales collateral.

By year three, Sam's company had hundreds of customers active on the platform, and Sam knew every one of them personally. So, when customer service levels dropped, Sam was the first to hear about it. She knew that it only takes one bad customer experience to impact the company's reputation negatively. Sam spoke to her leadership team about this early indicator. She requested a full proposal on solving the support level issue. Given her close relationship with her team, they immediately dug in. No one wanted to disappoint Sam. The support issue was fixed quickly and the company's stellar reputation remained intact.

Does Your Company Own Its Reputation?

Founders most adept at owning their reputation are often described as *people* people. While you may not know every employee, vendor, and customer by name, your company must have a mechanism for fostering relationships. How your company is viewed is foundational to attracting talented staff, eager investors, and loyal buyers.

The first place to focus on to assess if your company Owns its Reputation is to look at the current company culture. If the work atmosphere is something that has been put on the back burner, it's reasonable to expect that it may burst into flames somewhere down the line due to neglect. Company culture will develop, either intentionally with your input or unintentionally—and the latter will most likely not be favorable to your business goals. As the founder, how you relate to your staff is the heart of your brand and overall reputation.

Companies that Own Their Reputations love being adored by their employees and customers. They build deep relationships with both and keep these relationships at the center of their decision-making process. This is the core competency of the Connector. How would you assess your company in this regard? Are your employees and customers positively engaged? Are they deeply attached to the company's mission? Would they walk through fire to see the company succeed?

At my first company event at Side, CEO and fellow Connector Guy Gal offered to walk around and introduce me to partners and employees throughout the event. He stopped every thirty seconds to hug someone and introduce me by name to whoever was in front of us. He knew hundreds upon hundreds of people intimately. There were smiles on their faces as we walked the halls. He was happy to explain what each person did, often remembering their birthdays, spouses' names, and recent trips that they had taken. Not only were people touched by this, but they would also hand him gifts to express their appreciation for him.

How can your company Own its Reputation and help you acquire happy employees and happy customers? First and foremost, understand that the two have a deep connection. Spend time mindfully planting the seeds to grow both from the very beginning. Worded differently, you must appreciate the fact that how your company is viewed by the outside world is directly connected to how you and your staff relate to each other and the customers you serve.

Learn what a Connector knows: Your company's most important customer touchpoint is your employees—all of them. It isn't limited to your sales and customer success teams. It includes engineers, product people, finance teams, and janitors if you have them. Not only does everyone talk to people about the company they work for, but how you treat each other has a way of leaking into conversations about how your company treats customers and prospects.

Making certain employees show up positively to customers starts with setting an intentional culture. Companies that Own Their Reputations define their culture from the very beginning. It's vital to recognize that there is an unspoken set of shared values when you get a group together, no matter how small. These companies identify their values early on, immortalizing them with every employee and ensuring that decisions and communications live up to those values daily. If someone at the company doesn't model those values, they stick out like a sore thumb and do not last long within the organization.

But companies who Own Their Reputation don't stop there. They also define their brand and perfect the message to control

> **"**
> Learn what a Connector knows: Your company's most important customer touchpoint is your employees—all of them.

how the company shows up to the industry it serves. Brand is your company's personality, your belief system, and how you want the market to perceive you. It's about creating a consistent understanding of what your company represents. It is intentional and lays the groundwork for everything that you do.

If you focus on building positive relationships, your brand identity will emerge long before anything is put down on paper. While you might be tempted to ignore the larger industry in which you do business, you will have a better handle on your brand and reputation in the long run if you invest in connecting within your industry at the beginning or even before you launch your startup.

What might seem like small talk, wasted energy, and effort is actually a fact-gathering mission. People in the industry are the test center for your messaging. It's wise to go out into the world and try on all potential talk tracks with the people you know and trust. Then, share this newfound knowledge with the team to further refine the brand narrative that the company shares on its website, in its sales pitch, through advertising, etc. Gain a firm handle on what works and what doesn't. Once you've this nailed, you can guarantee it is consistently deployed across every channel.

Owning your reputation is an active daily choice to build and protect what you have built at all costs. Creating values and defining your brand identity are one-time initiatives. Still, companies that Own Their Reputations constantly monitor the actions taken against these identities at all times. That is essential since this reputation is what you will use openly to persuade new customers to do business with you.

If people have consistently positive experiences with your employees once they become customers, they

"
People want
to hear from
others like them.

will become advocates, sharing that experience with other potential customers. People want to hear from others like them, and if you have a great reputation, that advocacy will help you grow the business exponentially.

The Importance of Brand

You know you have a brand with intention when you recognize the brand personality by looking at the sign hanging outside the bathroom door. And that is exactly what you get in sunny Southern California when you visit the Boingo Wireless office. This small detail is as much for the guests who visit the office as it is for reminding employees that the Boingo consumer brand is fun, friendly, savvy, and even a little irreverent.

Boingo didn't always have this reputation. When Dawn Callahan, Chief Marketing Officer at Boingo Wireless, joined the team, it was a startup that had just completed its Series C round of funding. Boingo launched in 2001 with the belief that one day, Wi-Fi would be embedded into just about everything. It sounds obvious now, but back then, Wi-Fi wasn't even built into laptops and there were fewer than 400 public hotspots in the world.

Dawn started from scratch to build the brand with the understanding that nascent technology is more readily adopted when it feels approachable. So, Dawn and her team went to work to ensure that every single touchpoint – whether that was witty advertising copy, the friendly way customers were greeted in the call center, the irreverent types of swag handed out, or the fun office design (including those bathroom doors) – was treated as an opportunity to reinforce the brand personality.

Boingo's brand helped propel the company from startup to the world's leading indoor connectivity provider. Today, some 20+ years later, Dawn and the Boingo marketing team still lean into Boingo's fun, friendly, and slightly irreverent brand personality to set Boingo apart.

What Happens to a Company that Doesn't Own Its Reputation?

Your company's reputation can make or break your business, so having a Connector that Owns Your Reputation is critical to survival. If you have a poor reputation, inside or outside the building, it not only makes it hard to hire new employees and win customers, but it can also hinder your ability to retain them overtime.

According to a Harvard Business Review study [Chamberlain & Zhao, 2019, para. 7], each one-star improvement in a company's Glassdoor rating corresponds to 1.3 points out of 100 improvements in customer satisfaction scores. Why? Because your employees are your biggest brand touchpoint. So, if one of your company values is to care deeply for one another, and you have an employee who treats customers like support tickets, your brand reputation will suffer. If you have a value of transparency, and your employees don't feel like you share what is happening behind the scenes, they will complain either directly to customers or to people who know them. Even worse, the employees may become so disengaged with the business that your customers and prospects feel it, and your brand's reputation ends up paying for it.

Sure, some companies grow successfully despite their reputations, but it is an upward battle. They may hire a bunch of salespeople and then get frustrated that they cannot convert prospects into customers. Part of the reason this occurs is that the sales team is calling leads who have never heard of the company and have no opinion, positive or otherwise, about what the company does. Or worse, they have heard negative things about the company and want nothing to do with it. Imagine a world where those same prospects had heard positive things about your company. They not only had some awareness but there was so much buzz in the industry about you that they had already developed a very positive perception of your brand. Even if they don't know precisely what you do, they are much more likely to pick up the phone when you call.

The truth is, if you are in business long enough, you will have reputation of some kind; it may just not be the one you want. If you don't define your culture and your brand values, someone else will, and you will lose control over owning your reputation. Hopefully, it will come from happy customers. However, more often than not, it is your competitors that define your brand when you aren't looking, and, as you can imagine, they have anything but your best interest at heart. To prevent that from happening, take the time up front to define your values and your brand early and tie them as closely as possible to your origin story to help it take flight. If you do, you will have a solid reputation that will take your company to the next level.

Airbnb is an excellent example of having a solid connection between company culture and brand. (ycombinator.com/companies/Airbnb)They started with a simple statement on the Airbnb careers page that summed up their work environment: "No global movement springs from individuals. It takes an entire team united behind something big. Together, we work hard, we laugh a lot, we brainstorm nonstop, we use hundreds of Post-It's a week, and we give the best high-fives in town." Their values are clever in nature but simple to understand and identify with. Here are the Airbnb values:

- *Be a Host* – Care for others and make them feel like they belong. Encourage others to participate to their fullest, listen, communicate openly, and set clear expectations.
- *Champion The Mission* – Prioritize work that advances the mission and positively impacts the community. Build with the long-term in mind. Actively participate in the community and culture.
- *Be a Cereal Entrepreneur* – Be bold and apply original thinking. Imagine the ideal outcome. Be resourceful to make the outcome a reality.
- *Embrace the Adventure* – Be curious, ask for help, and demonstrate an ability to grow. Own and learn from mistakes. Bring joy and optimism to work.

It is easy to see how these values connect so well with their brand purpose: "Creating a world where anyone can belong anywhere." A lot of the undertones in their values support this cause. The employees at Airbnb embrace these values and are constantly pushing the boundaries to deliver on that purpose. And Airbnb consistently shows up and delivers against that purpose. From new product features, to guest and host experiences, to ad campaigns—it is very clear that this is what they are all about.

Not convinced? Here are some stats: According to The Lucid-press State of Brand Consistency report in 2021, sixty-eight per-cent of companies found that brand consistency increased revenue by up to twenty-three percent. The Prophet Brand Relevance Index shows that most relevant brands have outperformed the S&P 500 average by twenty-eight percent from a revenue growth perspective over the last decade. (Purewal, 2018)

So, if you would rather go to the dentist than spend inordinate amounts of time taking employees and customers to lunch, you will want to bring on a Connector who will build your reputation one conversation at a time. Your company's growth will depend on it. Without a Connector in the mix, each Superpower will make mistakes that could lead to a bad reputation. Let's explore each Superpower's assumption related to reputation and the errors that will likely follow.

To Build Brand, Start With Your Origin Story

Weddings. One of the happiest moments in a couple's life together.

On the other hand, preparing for a wedding can be stressful. In addition to crazy coordination, most couples want to look their best, so they set out to lose weight prior to the big day. That was the case for Mike Lee and his soon-to-be bride leading up to their beach wedding in 2003. As Mike explained (Lifehacker, Orin, 2014), they hired a fitness trainer who gave them a book listing the nutritional values of over three thousand foods and a pad of paper to track their calories.

For Mike, this seemed archaic. He had been a programmer since he was ten years old. He searched and searched the internet, but every digital option on the market was just as painful and time-consuming as manually logging his efforts in the notebook. So, he built his solution. He shared the app with family and friends and received positive feedback. Then, it began to spread by word of mouth. Fast forward to 2015 when MyFitnessPal was acquired by UnderArmour for $475 million and today boasts over two-hundred million users on the platform.

Regardless of your startup's stage at the moment, it is guaranteed that, like MyFitnessPal, your first few clients came from conversations with you, the company's founder. During these initial discussions, you told your story about why you started the company and shared your vision for your product and the future. Those initial customers jumped in right away, inspired by the mission and purpose being presented.

As your company began to grow, new employees entered the scene and began to share your founder's story. And now, as the company continues to grow, you put more and more people in front line positions that are further removed from you on the daily, and the origin story slowly starts to disappear. It happens slowly, and if you aren't careful, you may wake up one day, and your origin story is gone from your company's outward message.

You may ask, "So what? As we get bigger, is it *that* important? Shouldn't we be relying on the value that our products bring to customers and less on why the company was established in the first place?"

Letting your founder's story disappear is one of the biggest mistakes you can make, as it is the source for keeping your company's passion alive. Not only does this story give employees purpose, but it has the power of connecting deeply with customers for years to come. Some companies' origin story is so deeply woven into their brand identity that it never goes away. That isn't to say that it will be where you start every conversation, but it needs to be at the heart of your messaging forever.

Think of it as your company's soul or your true north. When you are faced with hard decisions along the way, you want to go back to it and make sure the commitments are supporting your original *why*. And that original *why* is tied to your origin story.

The sad truth is that when the brand concept comes in too late in the game, the origin story has already begun to dissipate, and customer and prospect perceptions have morphed into something else. The people you bring in to focus on establishing your brand will be looking more at who you are now versus where you came from, losing all that rich inspiring story along the way.

———

An Innovator's Mistake:
All I Need is a Cool Product

Innovator Jane certainly had a lot of friends who held sales positions within small to mid-sized sales teams, but Jane was not well known in the sales technology sector prior to starting her company. In the early days of gaining conviction, she leveraged these relationships to dive deep into their problems with current sales technology to understand where automation would be most beneficial. She didn't attend any technology conferences or get to know influential people in the space. Given her intense focus on the additional value she was creating, it didn't occur to her to do that. It isn't that Jane was not aware of all the players; she was plenty aware from the competitive research she did prior to building her solution. But the people involved, outside the customers themselves, were kept at arm's length.

When Jane launched her product, all her former colleagues were ready to sign up. Within the first year, her pilot customers were reporting significant efficiency gains, giving her company incredible case studies with actual metrics they could quote when speaking to prospects in their pipeline.

One of her initial customers was well-known and often quoted in the news. During a media interview, she spoke highly of Jane's solution, which landed Jane's company in the public eye for the very first time. Her competitors took notice. Even though Jane and her team only had a few dozen customers at that point, her competitors felt threatened and started spreading rumors about her product and its inferiority.

With much larger teams and budgets, Jane's competitors made it extremely difficult for her company to gain traction. Every time a prospect mentioned a feature that a competitor had over them,

Jane rationalized it to her team. She knew they were serving a niche part of the market and had all the confidence in the world that they didn't need those bells and whistles to make an impact. In fact, from Jane's initial research, many of these features were not even used by customers! Jane kept her team focused on the roadmap, knowing those items would provide much more value than the "me too" features that prospects requested.

Jane was proud of the work her team was doing and made sure that every feature they developed was communicated openly to existing customers and prospects via their website and sales materials. While the feature list was quite impressive, it was hard for prospects to understand who the product was for and why they should use it. So, when competitors started playing up the features Jane's company didn't have, it was hard for prospects to understand Jane's limited focus. Eventually, prospects lost interest in Jane's product offering, feeling like it was short on features before they even tried it.

If Jane had a Connector on the team, she would have someone out in the industry showcasing the value of Jane's product and sharing how it was superior in every way because of its focus on solving real problems rather than rolling out bells and whistles that nobody wanted.

A Builder's Mistake:
If You Can't Track It, It Isn't Important

Rich the Builder was very numbers focused. He had a roadmap of initiatives for the entire organization, each with a quantitative measure attached. Everything Rich did was in service of predictable growth. His leadership team reflected this focus, each hiring their team with precise job descriptions, goals, and metrics for which each person was responsible.

When Rich saw employees in the hallway, conversations were always about the business—what the person was concentrating on and their progress toward their goals. If progress was not being made, Rich dug in and asked a dozen questions to understand the nuanced details of what was going on. This line of questioning put employees on edge, making them afraid that their jobs were on the line at any given moment.

As a result, people worked around the clock to deliver for Rich. They worked through lunch and into the late evenings to get things done. Rich's employees felt like they were on a production line in many ways. No one knew each other too deeply, often using Slack and other tools to ping someone when they needed something. People were burning the candle at both ends, silently getting frustrated with their situation.

Rich didn't notice the burn-out happening in front of him. He never really thought about how connected, or lack thereof, people felt to the company's mission—especially in the early days when they were hitting all of their goals. They had a predictable number of new customers and added a few more people to support their growing customer base.

One successful member of the team, who had developed solid relationships with their customers, started sharing their frustrations with the customers themselves. Word got out that Rich and the team were over their skis and were working their people too hard with little reward. This rumor spread like wildfire through Rich's customer base.

Rich didn't notice it until their net promoter score dropped on his executive dashboard. Rich was left scratching his head—there was nothing new that should have caused their NPS score to drop that extensively. They didn't have any major issues with their product, nor had they made any significant changes to their service levels. If anything, they had added staff to ensure everything remained the same.

It wasn't until one of Rich's infamous hallway conversations with a trusted employee that he discovered customers showing concern for the company's viability. At this point, it was too late. Their reputation amongst customers had been tainted and cancellations began to roll in.

If Rich had a Connector on his team, it would never have gotten this far. The Connector, who would know each employee on a deeper level, would have sniffed out the pending burnout long before it got this far.

A Persuader's Mistake: Prioritizing Skill Over Fit

Good old Joe the Persuader started his company a few years ago with a few close colleagues from his previous company. Like many startups, they began meeting in his converted garage, all sitting around a folding table together with their laptops and a whiteboard off the side. It was easy back then. They all shared the same vision. They were dedicated to their mission, collaborative, and always honest and transparent with one another but in a calm and caring way. If someone had an idea that strayed from the core mission, they would call each other out. Everyone had an equal voice, and they were more productive together than they ever thought possible.

They were so productive that the business took off like a lightning bolt. Within the first ninety days post-launch, they had fifteen paying customers signed up and using their services. They were on cloud nine. By the thirtieth customer, they realized they needed to have someone running point on customer support. The founding team couldn't continue building the business and managing current customers. Luckily, Joe's niece had just graduated college and was looking for a job. They then had four people sitting around the table in Joe's converted garage.

The business kept growing and growing. At the end of year one, the team had outgrown the garage and rented a small office space to house their twenty employees. After all, business had been good. John and the team had just crossed the one-hundred-customer milestone! Their many employees spanned across multiple disciplines—sales, customer support, product, engineering, and operations. They were proud that all those employees had come from their networks. Joe often bragged about getting those highly talented and productive product and engineering folks to join his team because he had worked with them before.

Everything kept humming along. By employee number forty, they had all their favorite people inside the company. Now, they needed to double down on sales and support. No one knew any great candidates for these open positions. Katherine, the head of operations, posted the open job description on LinkedIn. Candidates came pouring in, and they began to interview them. Several were very qualified for the open roles. One in particular caught Katherine's eye. She had never worked with him before, but his face looked familiar. As she got halfway through the interview it dawned on her that he was the father of a boy on her son's soccer team. What a coincidence!

They instantly connected over that, and the operations manager decided to hire him. The Saturday before he started, she saw him yelling at the coach at a game. "Uh-oh," she thought. "I hope he doesn't get that heated at work!" It turned out he did. But it came from his passion for what he believed in, so Katherine didn't think too much about it. "People seem to like him for the most part."

Katherine moved forward and filled all the open support and sales roles. Everyone seemed to get along well, although it was like pulling teeth to get honest feedback from the sales team. It got back to Joe, and he was frustrated. In a leadership meeting with his founding team, he said, "It was so much easier to get things done when it was just us. Why is it that our team won't give us honest feedback? And the few times I have heard people try, that support guy gets fired up as if they are attacking him personally." He shook his head. "It doesn't make any sense."

Two weeks later, Katherine pulled together a report on trends in customer support tickets. She was surprised to see that overall satisfaction scores were significantly down from the previous quarter. For the first time, customers complained that changes were happening within the product that they didn't know about.

Upon investigation, Katherine was shocked to learn that some of her team was sharing their disappointment in how the product had evolved with their customers. This sentiment leaked out to the industry at large as customers talked to their peers who were at one point evaluating the product. What was a simple change that had been introduced to add value for their customers had now tarnished the stellar reputation they once had.

While this story is fictional, it illustrates that without a defined values system by which to hire, things can quickly get out of control. What seems easy in the beginning becomes cumbersome, and your ability to progress at the same speed as before gets significantly impacted.

Not only that, but once you have employees who don't fit your culture at the company, the overall culture of the company suffers. This has a way of getting out to customers, since your employees are your biggest touchpoints, and the reputation of your company can, unfortunately, follow suit.

If Joe had a Connector on the leadership team, culture would have been prioritized from the get-go, ensuring that everyone they hired after the first forty or so collaborated well with everyone else and provided a positive and supportive experience to his customers.

Reflections:

- Does someone in your company have the Superpower to Connect?
- Do any of the mistakes made by other Superpowers resonate with you?

On a scale from 1 to 10, rate the degree to which your company has Owned Its Reputation.

1-2	No, we're in trouble
3-5	Some, needs attention
6-8	Good, could improve
9-10	Great, it's the best thing we do!

1	2	3	4	5	6	7	8	9	10

CHAPTER 7

Win Customers:
The Superpower of Persuasion

*"You can exert no influence if you are not
susceptible to influence."*
—Carl Jung

Joe is the ultimate Persuader. Not only did he convince some former colleagues to join his new endeavor with very little pay, but his story was so compelling that venture capital firms threw money at him before he had anything to show for their investment other than his confidence in the opportunity ahead.

As the company began to take shape, Joe was the main point of contact on every vendor contract and every potential customer opportunity that came their way. Within ninety days of going live, Joe contracted fifteen-plus paying customers, with dozens more waiting in the wings. He was a master at using data to close the deal, taking the success stories from his current customers to sign up more. The company multiplied with Joe at the wheel.

As the business continued to grow, Joe brought on a small team of like-minded sales professionals to win customers faster and taught them his formula for success. Customers seemingly dedicated to his competitors appreciated the real-world success stories that Joe and his team told—so much so that they left decade-long relationships with other vendors to try Joe's solution.

When Joe's finance team had concerns about vendor costs creeping up to service the product, the team under Joe's leadership negotiated the prices to something more manageable. By keeping costs down and signing up customers at a decently rapid pace, Joe's company was able to hit its gross margin goals by the end of year one.

Does Your Company Win as Many Customers as It Should?

While all four of the G-R-O-W competencies are required to take your company from startup to GrowUp, an argument can be made that being able to sell your product and bring in revenue is the most important. So, let's look at your company to see if you are successfully winning customers.

Are you adept at closing? Are you a "sign on the dotted line" type of person? Do you create a win-win solution?

A company that Wins Customers has staff that can use charm and charisma to learn what makes people tick so that they can influence the decision-making process at every step. As the founder, it is imperative to create a company that believes anything is possible. This requires a compelling proposition and the right relationships.

A winning belief isn't limited to customer negotiations; it must be a standard with every action taken throughout the company's journey. The ability to persuade is a prerequisite when interacting with a customer, an employee, a vendor, or an investor.

Companies that are good at winning customers are strategic and analytical when approaching the world. They get to know their customers deeply and use the appropriate customer stories and proof points to overcome objections.

How do you measure your ability to close the deal? How do you articulate your sales method and strategy? Are you and your staff aware of all the chief decision points a potential buyer makes to hand you their hard-earned money?

> **"**
> Create a company that believes anything is possible.

Data as King

Regardless of the industry you serve and whether you are a business-to-business or business-to-consumer company, data is one of the most powerful things you can have in your arsenal, especially when you combine data with powerful customer stories. Those two items together can help your company punch way above its weight by securing media coverage in the various outlets that your target audience reads while also giving your marketing and sales organizations robust statistics to reference for prospecting. You can use these statistics in downloadable whitepapers, blogs, your website, and all your sales collateral to add credibility.

Data comes in all shapes and sizes. Suppose you have enough customers and are set up to track their success metrics. In that case, you can use your proprietary data to make the news. That said, not everyone has proprietary data at the onset of building a company. If you don't have internal data that is newsworthy, the best thing to do is make the news by surveying your target audience on a topic that is relevant to your business.

Think about this tactic for your own company. Is there a problem you are solving for your target audience that you could study and bring to the surface with data you could promote? It could be as simple as knowing what percentage of your target audience has the problem you are solving.

———

Like the Builder, Persuaders have a love affair with data. However, the type of data and how it is used can be very different. To Win Customers, you only need data that tells a positive growth story. While this can come from the same pool of metrics that the Builder tracks, such as customer growth, utilization, satisfaction, and the like, it can also come from customer case studies and third-party research. This data type allows your company to wax poetic about the customer that doubled their business by using your product or services or quote stats and anecdotes about how well your product solves real-life problems. Winning Customers is about finding the right data points to overcome objections and communicating your value proposition with such belief and confidence that customers cannot stop themselves from signing on the dotted line.

Why do companies who Win Customers detail out the buyer's journey? To identify all the things in the customer's life that will influence their decision to buy. Whether that influence is another person, an article, a podcast, or some other form of media, it's important to quickly surface this information in a single conversation and store it away for use in closing the deal when the time comes.

For example, when I first got to Side, a brokerage technology platform for top real estate agents to create their own companies, we didn't have the buyer's journey mapped out. We had the messaging dialed in after thousands of sales pitches, but how to reach these top real estate professionals beyond cold calling had not been thought through. We immediately started a project to interview as many customers as possible. We segmented those interviews by a few factors—those agents who were part of large teams rather than smaller teams, those who had been partnered with Side for years instead of months, and those who were in various metro areas across the country.

We generally found that those first movers with Side, the trendsetters and visionaries, constantly educated themselves on what was new in real estate and what was happening outside the industry. They were not only going to conferences within the industry, but they were also asked to speak at them. They were more apt to read and follow influential leaders outside of real estate, such as Richard Branson or Elon Musk. Their goal was to get in front of this segment and be inspired. Inspiration was going to be key. Sharing stories of high-profile agents like them would be motivating, alongside leadership books, speaking at conferences beside them, etc.

The agents we spoke to who were newer to the platform were more pragmatic. They were all-in on the real estate industry, followed top agents who shared tips on social media, and attended webinars or in-person events focused on skill training, such as generating leads or growing teams, which would be more up their alley.

The thing that cut across both segments was this pattern of education or leveling up. So, the most effective strategy for Side to get out in front of the industry and drive awareness and consideration was to get Side known as a top thought leader in the space. This strategy was most interesting because it was a bit of a "white space" opportunity, meaning that very few other companies were using that tactic. Most real estate vendors are quiet, and real estate events aren't as mature as those in other industries. That became the opportunity for Side to break out and get known in a meaningful way.

That is the power of a buyer's journey map. Once you have done the research, how to reach your target audience becomes crystal clear. As you can see above, you are looking for the best way to get in front of your audience at any stage in the purchase cycle, but you are also learning about the white space that not everyone else has taken advantage of yet.

Companies that win the most customers even go beyond the buyers themselves and look at the entire ecosystem and the data that will be required to win everyone over. They know what they want their company to look like two or three years from now and start with that end in mind. Their go-to-market plan includes key influential customers, vendors for distribution, new products or services needed to grow, and other influential people in the industry they serve.

At Roadster, the go-to-market (GTM) strategy was both top-down—extensive corporate relationships at the auto manufacturer level—and bottom-up—individual dealerships that hold influence in their market. We knew how crucial relationships with the auto manufacturers would be in order to get buy-in from the paying customers (the dealerships) long term, while there were no certifications.

Yet, for our type of software, there were other categories of software that the manufacturers certified and recommended for their dealerships. We started building relationships with the manufacturers right away, long before we had any business to do with them. We then evaluated our target customer and understood how influential big dealerships in each market were on both the auto manufacturers and other dealers. By targeting the most influential dealers, we were able to gain a win/win—the attention of the auto manufacturers and tapping into the "me too" of other dealers who watch these top performers' every move.

Last but not least, we also identified other people of influence in the ecosystem, like consultants and additional vendors serving our target customers. We made sure that they all knew who we were and had a deep understanding of our product offering. We gave them data they could use in their businesses to provide additional value. They quickly became advocates on the front line, organically mentioning us to their clients. We never paid them to do this; we just built relationships along the way. We knew the strategy was working when customers would mention that so-and-so told them about us.

Getting to Know the Industry Influencers

Don't ever underestimate the power of relationships throughout the entire industry that your company serves, not just your target audience. If someone reaches out to connect with you and they are in your industry, take the call. Get to know the other vendors that serve your same target audience, consultants, and competitors. All of these touchpoints add to your brand's reputation in the space.

If you don't know the players, don't be afraid to reach out cold to the people you surfaced in your GTM strategy planning. People like to feel important and valued. Let them know your company is new but that you have heard so much about them from others who respect them in the industry and would highly value their feedback on what you have built. When you tell someone they are important and their opinion is highly valued, you will be amazed at how responsive they are.

Once you have met with them and shown them your product or service, assuming they are impressed, you will have created an advocate in the industry. Whether you know it or not, they will be out there talking about you, recommending you, and perhaps even sending business directly to you. The interaction will be positive, and they will walk away thinking you are brilliant for asking them to help you.

While this may seem like a nice strategy when you have extra time on your hands, not doing it can come with a cost. If you are new to an industry and your target audience starts asking people if they know about your company, the last thing you want them to hear is that they have never heard of you. Worse yet, they have, but you are so small that they recommend being careful about doing business with you. The ecosystem could sabotage an unknown player without even realizing it.

What Happens to a Company that Cannot Win Customers?

A company will not be able to GrowUp unless it can win customers. It may have some initial success, but will take a herculean effort to grow at anything other than a snail's pace without the ability to combat formidable objections with compelling stories and data. When you grow too slowly, your company will be inefficient, meaning the cost to acquire a new customer will wildly outweigh the revenue you make from those you sign. That may be okay for a while if you raised a lot of money, but scaling the company to be profitable or go public means doing so in an efficiently. Even if you manage to keep costs low, your lack of growth could leave room for your competitors to take market share, thus edging you out of the industry over time.

The core competency of Winning Customers goes beyond the literal sense of the word "customer." It includes winning over the right employees, vendors, and investors. If you do not have a Persuader on the team, you will have a more challenging time getting what you need in place at a reasonable price. Sure, that star employee may join the company. However, they will require a crazy salary, and the vendor you need to do business with will still sign the contract—just not on favorable terms. None of this is impossible without the Persuader, but building a company that is as efficient as possible may be out of reach and will impact your bottom line.

This is not to say that companies without Persuaders do not win any customers. The Innovator will attract quite a few customers from their initial research phase but lose that momentum as the company sails into unchartered waters. An Innovator who can't close is just someone with great ideas. They may inspire some followers, but they won't be able to reach the masses.

The Builder translates the dream into processes with the needed licenses, financial strategies, policies, and procedures. They will build a sales team that produces a small but predictable number of deals based on the repeatable process of their top producer. But it takes the power of a Persuader to convince the masses to take a risk, whether that risk is investing in the company, joining the team, or signing up as a customer.

Connectors are the relational center of everyone involved, but most Connectors can't close deals. If they do close a deal, it isn't because of the product or service, it is because the customer trusts the Connector to give them a good deal.

While a good reputation and strong relationships is essential, it takes the Persuader to turn these connections into a significant number of customers who will purchase the product for the product itself.

If you are in business, you will have employees and customers; but it may not be the caliber of employee or volume of customers you need to accomplish your long term goals. To prevent this from happening, take the time to identify stories and positive data points your team can leverage in conversation with the people you need to influence. Ideally, hire a Persuader with the charisma to confidently leverage these stories and data points to scale your customer base while keeping costs low.

Without a Persuader on the team, the other Superpowers are bound to make mistakes that can have a material impact on your ability to convert customers and grow revenue. Without revenue growth, it is impossible to GrowUp. Let's look at the mistakes each Superpower will make without the Persuader by their side.

An Innovator's Mistake:
All the "What" without the "Why"

Remember Jane the Innovator? When Jane started her company, she focused on building technology to automate the typical sales process. Her founding team consisted entirely of product designers and software developers—all of whom had previously worked with Jane. They knew from years of observation and a ton of conversations with sales professionals in their network that their technology platform would transform the way sales teams operated across a plethora of different industries. And it did, for the first fifty-plus customers that Jane and her leadership team brought on.

Customers were delighted with their product offering as well. That fueled Jane and her team to build new features and functionality even more. Her initial customers applauded them. These customers were huge advocates who loved having a seat at the table when it came to product feedback and developing new bells and whistles that would make them even more productive in their day-to-day sales jobs.

Now there were so many great features, all of which Jane and her team thought were critical for a customer to be successful. Her team built out sales collateral summarizing each feature and how it worked. Jane was proud of these materials as they displayed how her product could do ten times more than the competitive products. She felt that the details of their materials highlighted her teams breadth and depth of knowledge about the space.

Given all the research they did, Jane was confident in her new product. She couldn't understand why her sales team had difficulty signing new customers after all her success their first year of business. Her sales team kept asking for some proof points they can use to overcome objections, but Jane and her team had yet to prioritize tracking so that they could understand the benefits quantitatively.

So, even though Jane always heard that the data would be helpful, reporting on new features that would make their customers more efficient was deprioritized. In the end, Jane had a more efficient product than anything else on the market but couldn't prove it to win over new customers.

If there was a Persuader on Jane's leadership team, sales wouldn't have waited around for reporting, they would have asked customers directly for the data they needed to include in their sales pitch. These case studies would have served as proof points to close deals. Not just that, but these case study wins would show Jane the power of having data, eventually convincing her to build out the reporting system needed to win even more customers.

A Builder's Mistake: Data Alone is Not Compelling

Rich the Builder had brought a product to bear at the right time to gain market share from similar solutions in the marketplace. He had spent time studying the reasons why customers purchased his product, including the success data from his top customers, and built a sales process that grew his revenue steadily within the first year he was in business.

By the end of year one, Rich was ready to hire a sales manager to catch all the incoming demand. Since sales itself was not Rich's forte, he hired Kevin, who had a wealth of sales experience. Not only was he a recommendation from his head of operations, but he had managed large scale enterprise teams for over twenty years! He thought to himself, "Thank goodness! I won't have to be in sales. I can spend one hundred percent of my time analyzing the business."

Kevin seemed great at first. He was operational by nature, and once he built a small sales team, he showed Rich how he tracked everything. Each person who made forty to fifty calls daily struggled to close new customers at the same rate Jane could early on.

Meanwhile, a large technology company in the space developed and began to sell a similar offering. Rich called them "ankle biters" and brushed them off during an all-hands meeting. No one took the established company seriously, even though they already had thousands of customers using that adjacent product.

Rich's product was superior in every way. Although the price point was competitive, the established company gained market share quickly, more than doubling Rich's customer count in less than a month.

Rich had failed to see early on that he needed a Persuader with storytelling skills on his leadership team. He didn't need a Builder as his head of sales sufficed at that early stage in the company's life. But if he'd had a Persuader in the mix, he would have a closer who could convince a significant part of the target market that their product was superior.

A Connector's Mistake:
All Talk and No Action

Sam the Connector built a product offering based on the biggest buzzword in the industry—Artificial Intelligence. She was determined to prove how much more efficient it would make people in the industry that she knew and loved. When it came to employees, everyone wanted to be on the ground floor with Sam because they believed in her greatness as a thought leader. Many of her initial customers came in on the ground floor too, with several of them investing in the company because of Sam.

Sam was a legend in the making. Her sessions at conferences were always packed. People loved her ideas and flocked to her for advice, but while she ran her own company, she rarely touted her solution as the answer to their problems. If someone asked her to explain what her company did, she was happy to provide an overview and even a demo if they really wanted it, but rarely pushed them to sign up. Instead, she used her influence to inspire people, regardless of which product they ultimately bought.

When an industry friend showed interest in learning more about her software, Sam introduced him to Jonathan on her sales team. Sam liked Jonathan since he also came from the same industry and was relatively well known. In fact, Jonathan was one of the first people Sam recruited to her new company. She met him at a conference a few years before. After he spoke on a panel, a line of people were waiting to chat with him. At the time, Jonathan was heading sales for a leading company in the space. Sam was impressed with him from the beginning and knew that one day he would be a sales leader for whatever company she started.

When the prospect met Jonathan, he was immediately put at ease. Jonathan took the time to get to know him and his business. They had lunch together many times over the next few months and became fast friends. Jonathan even recommended other tools for the prospect to use in his business. Still, after six months of building the relationship, the prospect had yet to become a customer. Jonathan was convinced it would eventually happen, and Sam agreed. Yet, it never did.

Jonathan was a Connector just like Sam. If she had hired a Persuader, the prospect would have had all of the data and case studies he needed to see how the software would have helped him run his business more efficiently. As a result, the prospect and hundreds of others would have signed on the dotted line already.

Customer as Hero

Have you ever been to a conference where the host forces you to endure a round of vendor speed dating? I have been to dozens of events where this has occurred throughout my career, but one, in particular, has always stood out. I was in Florida, the home of all marketing conferences—or so it seems—and was looking for a vendor to help with video production. It was one of the rare times I went to a conference looking to learn more than just best practices or be inspired by other marketers. I was on a mission to ask other attendees questions about their video capabilities and associated vendor partners. In theory, I was the ideal candidate for speed dating with vendors who could fulfill my needs.

Yet, as I walked up to the registration booth and over-heard the requirement to pick vendors for speed dating, my stomach turned, and I let out a sigh. I didn't want to be sold to. Truth be told, I hate being sold to. I always have. The more someone pressures me to buy from them, the less likely I will choose them as a vendor.

As a vendor myself, the irony is not lost on me. I was annoyed when I approached the desk and had to pick my three vendors. After all, I didn't want to hear from the vendors themselves; I wanted to hear from marketers like me who use said vendors. Still, I did my duty, smiled, and got through those vendor sessions.

Two hours later, I was sitting in a session listening to the head of marketing for a global consumer goods brand share her success story around a video campaign her company ran. Throughout the presentation, she talked about how her team crowdsourced this amazing video content and how much value they got for their budget. She talked about her vendor with such advocacy, describing them as a true partner and sharing the phenomenal results of their collaboration.

My ears perked up, and I quickly jotted down the name of the vendor she referenced. When I saw her at dinner that evening, I went out of my way to introduce myself and pick her brain further about her experience. She gave me the name of her account lead and promised to make an introduction.

Was it the same company I did a speed dating round with? No. But the fact is that her experience and advocacy for the vendor she had used far outweighed the vendor that was there handing out swag and trying to demo their product to anyone who would listen.

That is not a unique experience. It is human nature. People don't want to be sold to, and they don't want to hear from vendors. Why? Because they want an unbiased opinion that isn't just sunshine and roses but includes the pros and cons of going with one provider over the next. Business people want to hear from people like them. Word of mouth is the ultimate verification because it is organic and does not come from the company.

However, there is an easy way to present this information to potential customers. Share stories from your existing customer base that illustrate how your product or service helped them solve their problems and become even more successful, thanks to your company, than they ever thought possible.

Start by interviewing existing customers to find out which ones speak convincingly and with adoration for your product or service but also have data that can be shared as a proof point. Often, it is the customer's personality that makes a great customer story rather than how much of your product or service they use regularly.

If you get a great quote from the conversation, document it and ask for permission to use it. Don't worry if they don't say exactly what you would have hoped. Take what they said and write the quote for them. Most of the time, you will find that your version with a few embellishments is how they feel, even if they didn't say those exact words.

In these stories, the important part of making the customer a hero is just that—make them the hero, not you. They had the problem and sought out a solution. This may seem petty, but it is vital. Fashioning them the hero makes the story sound less salesy, and the customer will be likelier to share it with others.

Brownie points if you can capture these stories on video. Why? Because now you have the customer speaking directly to the prospect without a filter.

Reflections:

- Does someone in your company have the Superpower to Persuade?
- Do any of the mistakes made by other Superpowers resonate with you?

On a scale from 1 to 10, rate the degree to which your company Wins Customers?

1-2	No, we're in trouble
3-5	Some, needs attention
6-8	Good, could improve
9-10	Great, it's the best thing we do!

1	2	3	4	5	6	7	8	9	10

PART III

WHAT FATAL OBSTACLE ARE YOU OVERLOOKING?

CHAPTER 8

What Are Your Blind Spots?

"We humans are better at pointing out the elephants in other rooms than in our own."
—Lex Fridman

Your company is your creation. You envisioned it, built it, gathered employees and investors to help you succeed, and convinced customers to buy what you have to sell. You can be proud of that. Not everyone can achieve their dream.

Yet, the odds are against you pulling this off to the desired degree. Those odds are truly sobering. As we discussed earlier, startups have a ninety percent chance of failing. Would you bet on a horse with a ninety percent chance of losing? Your answer has to be yes because you're the horse, and those are the odds.

Think of it this way: Imagine you're at a networking meeting and ten people there have started their own companies. These are intelligent, creative, energetic people who are devoted to making their companies work. Uncountable hours, financial sacrifices, and optimistic hopes have been invested. These are people who are used to winning. And yet, only one of you will succeed. Will that person be you?

This book is about discovering the answer to a founder's most significant question: *What is the secret to being one of the ten percent?* To increase your chances of success, you need to acknowledge the following:

- Founders tend to have one primary way of being in the world, even if they have many talents, and that is their Superpower.
- This Superpower has been sufficient to launch a successful startup, but for a company to GrowUp, it needs to have the core competencies of all four Superpowers in play.
- The solution, then, is to make the needed changes to your company as soon as possible.

Does that sound easy enough? Perhaps. But the fact remains that only a portion of talented, intelligent, and dedicated founders are able to lead their companies from startups to GrowUps. There is more to it than simple insight or a one-size-fits-all business strategy. There's something else that most founders overlook and misunderstand about this process.

I believe that the true obstacle that trips up nine out of ten founders isn't staffing, funding, vision, or product—it's the founder's point of view. More clearly stated, it's what the founder can't see, and therefore can't address, that undermines success.

> It's what the founder can't see, and therefore can't address, that undermines success.

Our conscious minds filter through the myriad of data around us so that we can focus on the most salient pieces of information. No one is fully aware of everything at any moment in time. I call the things that are outside of our awareness, the things we can't see, "blind spots." We all have them.

But for the purposes of our discussion, it's important to note that each Superpower has a specific blind spot that decreases the company's odds for long term success. Let me make this more personal. Your superpower has a specific blind spot that decreases your company's odds for long term success.

In other words, the level of your self-awareness is the strongest factor in whether or not your company will succeed.

The Differences Between Weaknesses and Blind Spots

We've all heard that "Every strength has an accompanying weakness." We naturally rely on our strengths and avoid or overlook things we don't do well. Most of us don't like to fail, especially founders of startups. Hence, avoiding addressing areas where we might appear weak or incompetent is easy. Here's a quick overview:

If you're an Innovator, you're the master of gaining conviction. You're an exceptional problem-solver and can inspire people with the power of your ideas. You're weaker in this area if you're a Builder, Connector, or Persuader.

If you're a Builder, you are great at turning ideas into reality because process is your contribution. Ramping up by putting all the pieces into place to run an effective company comes easily to you, and it's also rewarding and engaging. That's not what floats your boat if you're an Innovator, Connector, or Persuader.

If you're a Connector, you are gifted with social skills, enjoy getting to know other people, and are naturally more likable than the other three Superpowers. These are your weak areas and need some attention if you're an Innovator, Builder, or Persuader.

Finally, if you are a Persuader, you are great at closing a deal, always coming up with ways to convince people to agree with your plan of action and are more interested in the ends than the means. It's more difficult for you to get people to sign on the dotted line if you're an Innovator, Builder, or Connector.

Because of these weaknesses, every founder must come to respect what the other Superpowers offer and utilize those abilities in their companies.

What is a Blind Spot?

Blind Spots are subjects, skills, and/or abilities needed to run your company that you cannot see. Therefore, you ignore or have a bias against addressing them because you do not think they are important or even exist.

Blind Spots—the Ten Percent Difference

Blind spots are an entirely different matter altogether. A blind spot is the one thing that stands in your way of success. It is the source of the trouble you're having now and could make or break your company.

While your weaknesses *may* lead you to fail in effectively fulfilling your organization's needs, blind spots *cause* you to overlook certain needs completely. You can think about your weaknesses as the things always at the bottom of your priority list, while your blind spots are the things that never even make it on the list because you don't value the effort.

A blind spot can stop you from hiring the right people, cause you to disempower the most effective team, and even set you up to miss the opportunity of scaling at the precise time. Many of the founders I have worked with are initially closed to my advice when it hits on their blind spot—even if the action could save their companies.

Let's bring this home. The blind spot of your Superpower can create damaging behaviors that undermine your products and services, sabotage your financial well-being, create a toxic company culture, and disrupt customers' ability or willingness to buy what you offer. And the worst part about a blind spot is, well, you're blind to it.

Think about your blind spot as your Superpower's Kryptonite— the one thing that can weaken, if not kill, your company if you do not find the antidote. The good news is that the antidote is typically right in front of you, if you can grow your awareness to see it. It is generally the one person in your organization with the core competency you are trying to avoid.

So, how do you identify your blind spot if you cannot see it? There is one significant piece of evidence when determining your blind spot: You will most likely have a strong negative response to whatever lurks in it. There's a rawness to the response, sometimes even irrational—a reaction that isn't one that you usually have.

You might dig your feet in when you like working collaboratively. You could cut someone off

> **Think about your blind spot as your Superpower's Kryptonite—the one thing that can weaken, if not kill, your company if you do not find the antidote.**

in a conversation when you usually hear people out. You could go into black-and-white thinking and blame one specific person or department for the company's problems rather than be open to the complexity of the situation. You might do the exact opposite of what is needed simply because you're over-reacting, under-reacting, or failing to act altogether.

However, the most dangerous challenge for a company is when a founder cannot see the issue. You may not respond strongly to your blind spot because you refuse to even consider the possibility. That is where a founder is challenged to increase self-awareness. If founders continue to turn a blind eye to their blind spots, the company is likely headed toward the ninety percent of those who can't survive in the long run.

What to Do With Blind Spots?

Can you see how your Superpower's blind spots can be problematic as you grow? Not having a plan for handling various scenarios that could stand in your way can be troublesome. Awareness is half the battle. You need to get ahead of this to ensure you have all four Superpowers within your team. And you must spend enough time with your team to set them up for success rather than sabotage them.

There is no time when your blind spots are more at play than when you are hiring someone. If you are honest with yourself, thoughts and fears related to your weaknesses are already running through your mind before you even meet candidates for the roles you need to fill. You are tempted to find people with a Superpower like yours to fill these seats. Fight the temptation. You will need your opposite in place to accomplish your long-term goals.

Share your fears openly, and let your team observe you in action. Even better, confess that you have opposite Superpowers with some folks and embrace your differences. Do you do certain things that have helped keep the company at the forefront of innovation or on track to deliver? Bring these strategies out into the open. Sure, the new person may have unique ways and methods, but if you don't explain what has been successful to date and listen to them, talking through their new ways of thinking, they will always miss the mark in your book.

CHAPTER 9

Overcoming the Innovator's Blind Spot—Process

"A goal without a plan is just a wish."
—Antoine de Saint-Exupéry

Some of my favorite CEOs on the planet are Innovators. Why? Because they are full of interesting new ideas and draw me into their vision of a better future. Things happen quickly around them, so there's usually excitement. Sounds great, right?

Innovators love speed. They have energy to spare and can quickly get their organization up and running at a breath-taking pace. On one side, that's good news. But Innovators also have weaknesses that slow down the whole endeavor.

Three of the Innovator's Weaknesses

1. Difficulty Planning Ahead

Innovators are master problem solvers, but they may fear that stepping away from day-to-day ideation to grow the rest of the company will bring innovation to a halt. On top of that, they don't have the patience to create job descriptions, detailed timelines, or determine data measuring tools themselves. That takes too much time.

2. Getting Lost In the Vision

Innovators have a tendency to get lost in their ideas. They will easily invest time into strategizing new solutions for customers instead of setting up systems and procedures to service them. Ask yourself if you love discussing ideas and concepts, identifying patterns, and imagining what could be without being dragged into how it will get done? Do small improvements to what has been built bore you? Do employees who used to love your innovative ideas now look at you with glassy eyes when you share your most recent brainchild? Relentlessly proposing new ideas can lead to burnout of employees, even the most loyal and devoted.

3. Prioritizing Their Ideas Over Others

I don't want to offend any Innovators who might be reading this, but this is something you most likely need to face. Because Innovators are often the most confident of the four Superpowers, they assume people will think their ideas are fabulous. If the response isn't what is expected, the Innovator may reject needed suggestions for product improvement.

Furthermore, relying on their inner validation, they may not take the best care of their relationships with their teams or customers. As long as they know their idea will help solve their customers' problems, they are happy to move ahead at breakneck speed. This can seem offensive or dismissive to others, and needed relationships may suffer.

The Innovator's Blind Spot—Process.
Ultimately, It's About Speed.

The reason things move quickly for an organization founded by Innovators is that they prioritize speed over process. To an Innovator, putting processes in place is the kiss of death. Once they have intuition about solving a problem, they want to solve it quickly and move on to the next thing. In their minds, process is seen as something that slows everything down. They ignore it at all costs and will sabotage anything that looks remotely like it.

The goal of process is in direct opposition to what the Innovator values. Process is about creating systems that will result in the same outcome every time. Process is about checking all the boxes in an efficient manner to ensure everything gets done right the first time. These include but are not limited to policies and procedures that standardize all activities and relationships within the company.

Creative ideas can be generated quickly in the mind of an Innovator. In contrast, process is slow to create and even slower to implement. The Innovator's blind spot is everything that isn't conceptual, future-oriented, intellectually creative, and fast. Fast is the only speed accepted by an Innovator.

Innovators have an unrealistic view of time. How long does it take to produce the product or service? Is there a production plan? What are the steps, and who is responsible for those steps? These are questions Innovators are not only reluctant to ask but think are unnecessary complexities that slow teams down. "Just dive in and get things done," is how the Innovator thinks. For the Innovator, it's full speed ahead to get something out the door so they can either iterate from there or move on to the next innovation.

The Innovator's blind spot also impacts the structure of the company itself. If you're an Innovator, you have a clear vision that draws people in. If you are an Innovator, look at your company for a moment. Chances are very high that your company resembles a solar system with you as the sun and everyone else rotating around you. While most startups must begin with the founder as the leader, it will probably be a surprise that other Superpowers don't run their companies like you do. You can find out how they set things up when we cover their blind spots in the following sections.

With you at the center of your company's universe, you are the originator of the ideas and solutions and, chances are, the architect of all products and services. The entire company's growth plan is solution-led and rolled out with the speed in which the Innovator can imagine them—which are abundant. The Innovator takes off in one direction after another with employees trailing behind without clear guidance on what is expected of them and when. Let's dig a little deeper into this blind spot.

Anyone who tries to bring order to things will be met with massive resistance. With the Innovator at the center of the company's universe, there is no time to slow down. There are more ideas than can be implemented, and without a process to prioritize them or procedures detailing how to get things done, everyone gets frustrated by the lack of progress—especially the Innovator. If you're an Innovator, ask yourself these questions: Do I expect my team to execute most of my ideas as they come up? Do I have trouble letting people prioritize for fear that things won't get done? Do I overreact when an employee wants to slow down a beat and do things differently?

If letting go of how things get done is a strain for you, this blind spot can result in the opposite of speed—it can bring the company to a screeching halt as they try to juggle too many projects at once.

This blind spot can create conflict and discord in the company—especially Builders who are process-oriented and data-driven.

Builders are all about systems and structure. They are logical, fact-based individuals who value organization, process, and predictability. A Builder ought to be hired as your COO or head of operations, but you must let them do what they do best. This critical role enables you to do what you do best at scale for hundreds, if not thousands, of customers versus just a handful.

How you deal with other personality types will be critical. You will tend to fight the organization and the process orientation that Builders bring because it will feel like they are slowing you down when you want to be innovative and fast. You know in your heart of hearts that moving fast without the groundwork to scale properly will lead to ineffectiveness over time. Still, the fear of red tape is so deeply rooted that you fight them every step of the way.

The fatal mistake for the Innovator is organizing all of your decisions around speed. If process is seen as something that slows everything down, you will ignore it at all costs and will sabotage anything that looks remotely like it. You won't gather the data needed to make sales predictions. Employees will be without proper guidance and helpful feedback. Without paying attention to the outside world, not just the creative, joyful place in your mind, you'll be less likely to see danger on the horizon. When problems arise, as always, the Innovator can be completely unprepared, mentally and practically. Often running on the edge of financial viability, all it can take is one downturn in the economy or a season of unfortunate events, and the Innovator's dream is destroyed.

If you're an Innovator who has started an innovative company with solutions that people need, be forewarned. Addressing your blind spot can make the difference between being able to help your customers in new ways or joining the majority of companies led by Innovators that fail.

A Tale of an Innovator's Blind Spot

What happens when you focus exclusively on product development? When Jane the Innovator started her company, her entire team focused on building technology that would automate the typical sales process. Her founding team was full of product designers and software developers, all of whom had previously worked with Jane. They knew from years of observation and a ton of conversations with sales professionals in their network that their technology platform would transform how sales teams operate across various industries. And it did at first.

Customers were extremely satisfied with their product offering, which fueled Jane and her team to pour even more into building out new features and functionality. Her initial customers applauded them. These customers were huge advocates that loved having a seat at the table when it came to product feedback and developing new bells and whistles that would make them even more productive in their day-to-day sales jobs.

As the volume of customers increased, so did the number of feature requests. Jane hired a head of product development to run the day-to-day operation so that she could focus on running the business. However, her new VP saw the number of new requests and began to put in processes and procedures to prioritize what could reasonably be done with the resources allotted.

Jane noticed that while the roadmap looked large, progress was slowing. She looked down on all of the red tape that her VP had put in place and felt the product development process had been over-engineered. She inserted herself back into the mix, peeling off a few engineers to work on a skunk works project that she felt would add a lot of value.

Not only did her new VP feel disempowered, but he had to prioritize further the number of bug fixes and enhancements they could deliver to their customers. When he went to Jane requesting more resources, Jane initially shook her head. She didn't understand why they couldn't produce the same output. She had to stop herself from blaming the VP for adding process and not inspiring engineers to work hard and meet the deadlines.

However, Jane had a new-found awareness of process as her blind spot, so she put her feelings aside and trusted her VP to add a few more engineers to the team. If she had not done this, progress would have slowed, leading customers to complain that the system needed to be fixed. Jane's company would have lost customers. They would have fallen behind the curve, opening the door for competitors to gain market share.

With additional engineers in place, Jane's company scaled the product team to innovate and handle the inbound feature requests and issues. The process that her VP put in place helped them prioritize the work, ensuring that they built only what was necessary to accomplish their goals. And they did just that. Within twelve months of scaling the team, Jane's company had gained ten basis points in market share.

Jane also gained a real appreciation for her VP's capabilities. She learned that his ability to build teams and process complimented her ability to innovate and inspire. Their partnership grew alongside their trust in one another.

Reflections:

- Do you or someone on your team have a blind spot related to process?
- How has this blind spot shaped the relationships within your company?
- Can you think of times when you or someone else on your team reacted poorly to process?
- Is there someone in your company being sabotaged for putting process in place?
- What would happen if they were empowered to implement process?
- How often do you have difficulty planning ahead?
- How often do you get lost in the vision?
- How often do you prioritize your ideas over others?

CHAPTER 10

Overcoming the Builder's Blind Spot—Risk-Taking

"You miss 100% of the shots you don't take."
—Wayne Gretzky

Let's be real. No startup on the planet can GrowUp without someone who can run the numbers and build process to scale—they can't GrowUp without a Builder. Builders are all about systems and structure. Because of that, they have a head start in a lot of ways.

If you're a Builder, you are a logical, fact-based person who values organization, process, and predictability. You have been grounded in hiring the right people, and your employees are clear on the details and expectations of their jobs. You're also a natural planner who puts process in place to ensure success. In all likelihood, you have laid out the entire company's growth plan. Sounds great, right? Well, there is that little thing called a blind spot that can trip up even the most prepared Builder.

The Builder's blind spot is anything that requires or even looks like it might require risk-taking. The need for predictability and control over every decision can push the Builder into a level of fear that jeopardizes the company. In contrast to Innovators, who often fly by the seat of their imaginations, Builders want to move slowly. They are concerned that cutting corners could lead to foreseeable failure.

The Builder's blind spot impacts the structure of the company created. The organizational chart most likely reflects a more traditional hierarchy with the Builder/Founder at the top and management reporting directly to the Builder. As the organization grows, new squares will be added below the management level, with everyone answering to the person above them. Are you a Builder who takes comfort when everything is clear and in order? If so, I must challenge you by asking if your company is really as safe as you want to believe.

Three of the Builder's Weaknesses

1. Difficulty Being Flexible

Let's take another look at the organization chart. It illustrates that employees don't have access to you—at least according to how it's "supposed" to work. If you're a Builder, it's important to notice that it will take time for an employee who has an innovative idea to get that idea heard. They will first have to go to their immediate supervisor. If cleared by that person, the employee may be permitted to go up another level in the hope of eventually approaching you.

But then again, there may be papers to fill out and a timeline to follow. The lack of organizational access and the inability to move more quickly can stifle creativity and innovation.

You might also slow people down to triple-confirm the decisions made by reliance on data. Once you figure out the "right" way to do something, you'll naturally make sure everyone is trained to do it that way every single time. While this ensures scalability to keep the trains moving the way they need to be, it can slow things down significantly, showing very little progress from a growth perspective at a time when rapid growth is expected.

2. Getting Lost in the Details

A second weakness is related to the Builder's love for planning and details. As a Builder, you probably love a project plan and a set of concrete goals.

Project plans and metrics are not things that typically inspire and motivate teams. It's important for you to realize that most people are motivated by the "why," and not the "how," which is the opposite of what energizes you. Inspiring people is a weakness that is important to address as the company expands.

3. Prioritizing People as a Means to an End

As a Builder, you aren't uncaring by nature. Still, you've probably said, "It's not personal. It's business," more than the other three Superpowers. You like people, but unlike the Connector, you're not prone to chatting in the office and getting to know people.

Instead, you will hire people based on tasks to be completed without taking into account how that person may fit or not fit into your company's culture. Since company culture is not a high priority for you, it's easy to be taken off-guard by how one particular hire can upset the entire company.

While execution makes people a catalyst for scalability, how you treat people can hinder harmony among employees, investors, and potential customers.

The Builder's Blind Spot: Risk-Taking. Ultimately, It's About Safety.

If there's a car speeding past you on the highway, chances are there is not a Builder at the wheel. Builders are not risk takers; they are naturally cautious, and, therefore, like to take life and business building slower than the other three Superpowers.

Since all Superpowers tend to hire people who match their strengths, your sales leader will be more science than art, your product teams will focus more on logical features than big wow moments, and you risk your reputation being unmemorable. Why? Because you need that scrappy, risk-taking startup streak in your company to accomplish your vision.

You will also be more cautious when it comes to decision-making. You like to use data to be sure things will work out the way you want them to. As a result, you may shy away from the big bets with uncertain outcomes when it's precisely those bets that can take your company to the next level. While taking risks that put the company in existential danger is

> **"** If there's a car speeding past you on the freeway, it is not a Builder behind the wheel.

not prudent, Builders falsely believe that doing risky deals is fool's gold. You may say, "Why invest energy into something unproven when you can get to where you want to go if you stay on the beaten path that is tried and true?"

The Achille's heel for the Builder is that their attempt to avoid all risk is the exact thing that will sabotage their success. A startup needs to be nimble and able to walk through a door of opportunity when it opens—not when it fits into the five-year plan. The product you developed may have been needed when it was designed initially, but if the market changes, you'll be slow to respond and become obsolete. We see that happen constantly in this quickly changing global economy.

When people in the organization want to take on an initiative with an unknown outcome, you will tend to question their judgment. You will often stop them in their tracks. It's not that you say no; it may be better if you did right from the beginning. Instead, you request so much proof before approval that the project eventually stalls out, and the employees lose their passion and are completely demotivated. When the team tries to go fast and fails, the Builder is the first one to point out, "If they had just spent some time analyzing the situation in depth, they would have known it wouldn't work." This is the way Builders can lose their most talented and creative employees.

Perhaps the most dangerous aspect of the Builder's blind spot is that your company takes too long to achieve demonstratable success. Investors may be disappointed at how long it takes for you to make a profit at your slow and steady pace. Your profit margin may be lower than you'd like while your employees complete scads of paperwork following the proper procedures. And customers are fickle. They go after the newest, shiniest object on the market. If they aren't excited about your product, there will be no profit.

A Tale of a Builder's Blind Spot

Rich is the Builder who grew his company's revenue steadily year after year and put all the processes and procedures in place to scale the business effectively as his revenue grew.

Rich was proud of the fact that he created such a predictable business. He had a strong leadership team who was masters at execution. His leaders had put the right people in place underneath them to make sure every initiative they took was completed on time and contributed to a measurable goal.

As the company grew, Rich's head of product development hired more and more product managers to guarantee they could keep a consistent pace toward their overarching goals.

Jackson, one of the newer product managers, came from the industry and had many connections. In fact, he previously worked for a company whose product was complementary to the one Rich's company had built. This sparked an idea. If they integrated the two products, it would streamline their customer's workflow. Maybe people would pay more money for that.

Jackson brought this up with his manager during their weekly sync-up. While it was an interesting idea, his manager asked a bunch of questions that Jackson couldn't immediately answer about the viability of this integration, ultimately telling Jackson to focus on the projects at hand.

Jackson continued to think about the integration. In his off hours, he talked to a few customers. He put together a well-thought-out proposal answering all the questions his manager originally asked him about. This time the proposal went beyond his manager to the head of product. A meeting was set up a few weeks later for Jackson and his manager to share the idea. The head of product wanted more data. After all, they couldn't prioritize an integration like this unless they knew for sure it would be more valuable than other items on the roadmap.

Everything they had built so far was proprietary. Integrating with someone else's product would open up the possibility of something going wrong. They would have zero control over this other company's actions. What if their system went down? Would their joint customers' unhappiness rub off on them?

When Rich got wind of the concerns, his initial reaction was to put the idea on the backburner. However, Rich was aware that he had a blind spot for risk-taking, so he encouraged the team to evaluate the integration further. They pushed through the concerns, started beta-testing the integration, and were pleased with the results.

Fast forward six months and an article was written about Rich's integration. Customers of other companies read the article and began to submit leads for his sales team to follow up on. The integration was such a success that the head of product development promoted Jackson to a full-time role, pursuing additional integrations for the company.

If Rich had not recognized his blind spot and empowered Jackson to take a risk, one of Rich's competitors would have pursued these important integrations. Given the existing agreements, Rich and his team would have been locked out of the vendor ecosystem, and when customers and prospects started demanding the integrations that competitors had, Rich and his team would have been behind.

Reflections:

- Do you or a team member have a blind spot related to risk-taking?
- How has this blind spot shaped the relationships within your company?
- Can you think of times when you or someone on your team reacted poorly to something risk-related?
- Is there someone in your company that is being sabotaged for risk-taking?
- What would happen if they were empowered to take risks?
- How often do you have difficulty being flexible?
- How often do you get lost in the details?
- How often do you prioritize people as a means to an end?

CHAPTER 11

Overcoming the Connector's Blind Spot—Empowerment

"Leadership is about empowering others to achieve things they did not think possible."
—*Simon Sinek*

Connectors play a special role in the industries they serve. With their connections, they use their Superpower to open doors for their companies that other types of founders dare to dream of for their own. They get to know people and are motivated to explore these relationships deeply. It is what makes Connectors great allies in the industries they serve. Connectors deeply understand the customer and, as a result, are best at positioning the company in ways that resonate.

Having a Connector at the top typically means your company has a stellar reputation—this makes it much easier for the sales department to close deals. Sounds great, right? And it is!

Yet, the Connector has a hard time letting go. For the Connector, it is all about staying on message no matter the consequences. If you're a Connector, you may be closed off to any new ideas that are not perfectly aligned with the company's current position in the marketplace. Controlling the brand and message is of utmost importance to you. And, if you're honest with yourself, you might be so invested because you are always center stage. For that reason, you may have a death grip on the company's strategy. How else can you ensure that everything remains aligned with the industry's perception of you?

The Connector's organizational chart might look like the Innovators, yet it's more like a fan club with you on stage and everyone else in the audience. You're probably the organization's "face," and you've utilized your founder's story to the maximum extent. Indeed, the other Superpowers have loads to learn from you in this regard. However, this need to be in control could ultimately lead to your company's demise.

Three of the Connector's Weaknesses

1. Difficulty Staying Objective; Closed to Input

Connectors are so laser-focused on keeping the company's reputation intact that they don't always listen to new ideas or consider new ways of thinking outside the box. This can be extremely limiting when it comes to growing the company, and if they aren't careful, it could lead to disempowerment and resentment amongst the employee base.

2. Getting Lost in the Relationship

A second weakness is their love for spending time with customers. Connectors love inspiring people with their ideas and stories, but they can get lost in relationship building and forget to close the deal. They have difficulty focusing on the details, often surrounding themselves with Builders who can bring their vision to life. However, this behavior leaves little room for others to contribute to the strategy at large. When the Connector is out of the office—which happens often to connect with the industry—negotiations and strategic decision-making will likely halt.

3. Prioritizing Appearances Over Integrity

Connectors' decisions are based on the impact it will have on your company's reputation in the ecosystem. Will this add or detract from what people think about you today? While this is great most of the time, it can limit the transparency you want to provide your employees and customers. Not everything at your company is rainbows and roses, but the Connector may spin the truth to keep it from tarnishing its position in the marketplace.

The Connector's Blind Spot: Empowerment. Ultimately, It's About Control.

The irony of our blind spots is that when we are overly invested in a particular goal, we sabotage the very thing we desire. If you're a Connector, you know how much you value how your brand shows up in the world. For you, it's the key to your long-term success.

> **"**
> A company isn't about one person. It's about building a team that can eventually go forward without you.

But you can get so lost in the vision and building goodwill that the opposite occurs. A company isn't about one person. It's about building a team that can eventually go forward without you. To move your startup to a GrowUp, you must empower people in your team. Unfortunately, your blind spot leads to refusing to empower others internally to share and execute their ideas. The brand must be a group effort, not simply your effort. You are the founder but not the star. Your staff is your team, not your entourage. Your business will die on the vine without relying on your team to close deals or meet other key performance indicators.

Connectors can bring a company's ability to execute to a halt with their perfectionist mindset. It isn't about deep analysis or process like the Builder, though. It is about seeing that every move is consistent with how the founder and the company are perceived in the marketplace. This need for control impacts the team's ability to do what it takes to grow the company. You hire people who will go along with what you want to do rather than creative people who want to make your company bigger and better. Afraid of competition within your own ranks, you'll likely wind up pooh-poohing ideas to drive the business forward if it may even, in the smallest of ways, impact the reputation you have artfully created.

As the company scales, the Connector becomes the bottleneck, trying to control what goes out to the industry. That makes everyone trying to create customer demand feel disempowered and frustrated with the red tape it takes to get anything done. Eventually, the Connector gets disgruntled by the fact that the team is missing a strategic point of view, forcing them to review everything. The company may fail simply because of the lack of process and the sheer unhappiness of the employees. But the Connector's blind spot will be in full display when, upon the founder's departure from the company, everything comes to an end.

A Tale of a Connector's Blind Spot

What happens when you become the bottleneck? Sam is a Connector who cares deeply about her employees and her customers. She spends an enormous amount of time with customers and is the reason the company has a great reputation. When her customers complain about support issues, Sam doesn't hesitate to hire additional employees to guarantee her customers are taken care of. And even though she has a support staff, customers tend to contact Sam when they have issues. They know Sam will always be on their side.

Sam hired a head of sales who quickly built out the sales team. While making inroads and signing customers, Sam discovered that each customer heard a different story about their company and what they offered. She was not pleased. Sam started to insert herself into the sales experience to rectify this, but the volume of sales meetings had significantly increased with the additional headcount. Given her desire to be in every meeting and having an already hectic schedule, their sales volume began to dwindle.

Sam realized what she was doing was not sustainable. Her blind spot got the best of her once again. Instead of working with her head of sales on the message and empowering him to assess his team, she was trying to take control. With lofty goals given by the board, Sam knew that she had to get out of the way and let her sales leader assess the team's performance and level up the team to keep the volume high. Otherwise, sales would have ceased, forcing her head of sales to significantly increase the sales team size to meet their aggressive annual goals.

However, enlarging the team would have made the bottleneck with Sam even worse. Instead of developing the top line, it would have significantly increased the rate at which they were burning money, making it harder to raise funds for continued growth. Without seeing the cycle, eventually, Sam would have run out of money and been forced to close her doors, leaving hundreds of customers and employees hung out to dry.

With a newfound awareness of her blind spots, Sam could step aside and let her head of sales do what he does best. After all, the team was closing deals and just needed some training to stay on message. Also, empowering her sales leader freed up Sam to build relationships with some of their newer customers, where she learned that they weren't getting as much value as her initial customers had. With a renewed focus on empowering her staff, Sam took this to her head of product development, who dug deeper into the issue.

Sam was impressed with her head of sales and head of product development. Both leaders addressed the problems without Sam's interference and the company thrived. She felt great about her team and gave them the recognition they deserved. With more happy customers in place came more and more word of mouth. Sam was tickled pink. Everyone in the industry had positive things to say about her company.

Reflections:

- Do you or someone on your team have a blind spot related to empowerment?
- How has this blind spot shaped the relationships within your company?
- Can you think of times when you or someone on your team reacted poorly to a decision that could have impacted your reputation?
- Is someone in your company being sabotaged for taking action without approval?
- What would happen if they were empowered to make decisions?
- How often do you have difficulty staying objective?
- How often do you get lost in the relationship?
- How often do you prioritize appearances over integrity?

CHAPTER 12

Overcoming the Persuader's Blind Spot—Consistency

"People like consistency. Whether it's a store or a restaurant, they want to come in and see what you are famous for."
—Millard Drexler

I have always been impressed with Persuaders. Their ability to wax poetic and gain buy-in from customers and employees alike is impressive. They are brilliant entertainers. For Persuaders, life is a story, and they love to have an audience to share it with. There isn't an objection that they can't overcome, which helps them win people over—customers and employees. They find it easy to hire whomever they set their eyes on, knowing they will personally win them over in the end.

Having a Persuader at the top means the company's growth plan is sales-led. The product is built on customer needs, and customers are happy because they feel heard. That is great initially, but what happens when your customer base grows, and the company can't keep up with the one-off requests from the field? You must scale your products and services to handle the masses. However, this won't be possible given the customizations made to please each customer.

As time passes, the Persuader's desire to please every customer makes it hard to scale products and support services. Let's take a closer look at what the Persuader is not good at.

Three of the Persuader's Weaknesses

Persuaders are natural storytellers who are drawn to people with similar characteristics. This can mess with their ability to hire the right people for the right roles, especially when it comes to Builders, who have a critical role in scaling the company due to their detail- and process-oriented mindset. Persuaders run the risk of sabotaging other's efforts with short-term needs and one-off customer requests if they do not stay present in this shortfall.

1. Difficulty with Long-Term Focus

Persuaders are extremely focused on the here and now, doing whatever it takes to close the deal. The Persuader will almost always choose the opportunity right in front of them since it is there for the taking versus an option that may take months or years to see come to life. When growing a company, it takes big-picture thinking and long-term focus to go the mile. So, while the Persuader may talk big, they get distracted very easily by the shiny object before them, taking the company and its employees on a detour.

2. Getting Lost in the Deal

A second weakness of the Persuader is their love of the story, which can easily slide into fantasy. If you're a Persuader, be aware that you might get too caught up in the yarn you're spinning. You might not intend to be deceitful, but you may promise more than you can deliver. You may also find it hard to stay on brand. Persuaders are chameleons and will say whatever it takes to close the deal. That can be very frustrating for the team that's putting guardrails in place to grow predictably. They cannot understand why the Persuader doesn't stay on script and just sell what they have available.

3. Prioritizing One-Off Customer Requests—Inability to Say No

As a Persuader, you may also have difficulty saying no to customers. As a result, the product queue gets clogged with one-off customer requests that do not align with features they may be building for the masses. As a result, innovation slows down, and the company slowly loses relevancy to other companies in the marketplace.

The Persuader's Blind Spot: Consistency. Ultimately, It's About the End Regardless of the Means.

Persuaders are people pleasers but only as a means to an end. Their "do what it takes" mentality is the basis for their blind spot—a natural outcome of using any means necessary results in a lack of consistency.

Here's how it plays out. Their goal is to convince the customer to buy the product or service. Relationships, then, are transactional in nature, with many of them being short-lived. If the Persuader is selling something that relies on repeat buyers, they will maintain a positive connection for the purpose of making another sale.

Customers, whether the connection is short-term or long-term, are highly valued given the Persuader's goals. Making the sale can eclipse the Persuader's loyalty to the company itself. In the pursuit of pleasing the customer, they may be less concerned about what others in the company are trying to accomplish and more concerned with getting things done on behalf of the customer.

Every customer comes with a different needs and wants, which propels the Persuader to accommodate different goals. Policies and procedures can be seen, not as requirements, but suggestions. Persuaders sometimes view rules as hindering efforts to success and, therefore, meant to bend, jump over, or ignore altogether. As each customer presents the Persuader with a different challenge, the method of describing, delivering, or pricing a product or service varies in each transaction. Anyone who tries to stop the Persuader from promising something different than what the company currently offers better be prepared for the Persuader's wrath.

If the Persuader is the founder, then the company as a whole can be jeopardized by the arrival of each potential customer. Employees may become confused about what is expected and frustrated over having to respond to ever-changing demands of the Persuader. Consistency is necessary for building a sustainable business. Still, Persuaders are so short-term focused that they derail consistency at every turn.

So, whether they are green-lighting a custom request to close a deal, trying to get people to work together without needed parameters, or going off script to get someone bought in, the lack of consistency will bite the company in the long run.

As the company tries to scale, the Persuader's blind spot will not deliver the consistency needed in all business areas to grow sustainably.

A Tale of a Persuader's Blind Spot

What happens if you don't focus on consistency as you grow?

Persuader Joe, who started his company with a few close colleagues from his previous company? As you may recall, his business took off like a lightning bolt and had fifteen paying customers within the first ninety days. They had so many paying customers out the gate because Joe convinced them to buy the product.

Joe was a master storyteller. Once they had one customer, he took that story and the success metrics from that customer to sign up other customers. That is how they multiplied with Joe at the wheel. But, as more and more people showed interest in their product offering, Joe began to hear all sorts of unique situations where a prospect was looking for a product to do this or that. To get these deals at the beginning of the company's life, Joe promised prospects that the product could solve their unique circumstance. As a man of his word, Joe would work with the team to add a custom feature to support these first many customers.

As the CEO, he could skip the line, constantly inserting new features into the product roadmap and continually delaying the bigger features that his team was working on to keep them ahead of the competition.

With a newfound awareness of his blind spot, Joe could see that this behavior might delay more significant features that would take his company to the next level. While he couldn't stop his customer-pleasing tendencies, he learned to not promise anything himself, leaving that to his head of product to assess and respond to.

If he had not gotten control over these promises, innovation would have slowed, and the competition would have leapfrogged them. The customizations would make it impossible to universally upgrade the platform and their market share would eventually dwindle to nothing.

While this is a fictional story, examples of this "do what it takes" mentality occur daily in businesses worldwide. Without consistency in what you say or sell, you can find yourself in a world that is not scalable.

Reflections:

- Do you or someone on your team have a blind spot related to consistency?
- How has this blind spot shaped the relationships within your company?
- Can you think of times when you or someone else on your team tried to enforce consistency?
- Is someone in your company being sabotaged for trying to make things consistent?
- What would happen if they were empowered to keep things consistent?
- How often do you have difficulty with long-term focus?
- How often do you get lost in the deal?
- How often do you prioritize one-off requests?

Part III: Summary Chart

Founder	Innovator	Builder	Connector	Persuader
Weaknesses	Difficulty planning ahead Gets lost in the vision Prioritizes ideas over people	Difficulty with being flexible Gets lost in the details Prioritizes people as a means to an end	Difficulty staying open to Input Gets lost in relationships Prioritizes Appearances over Integrity	Difficulty with long-term focus Gets Lost in the Deal Prioritizes One-Off Customer Request
Blind Spot	Process	Risk-Taking	Empowerment	Consistency

PART IV

WHAT PRACTICAL STRATEGIES ARE NEEDED FOR YOUR COMPANY TO THRIVE?

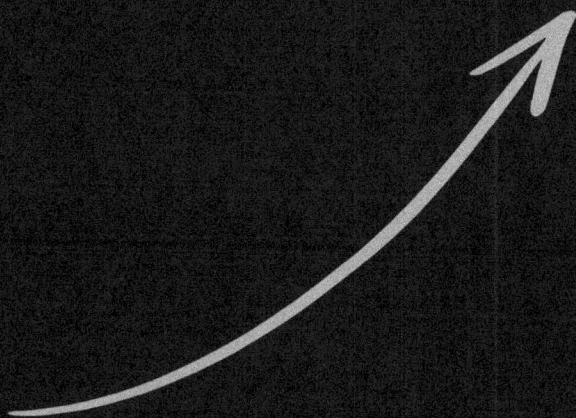

CHAPTER 13

Growing Your Company Starts With You

"The greatest superpower is the ability to change yourself."
—Naval Ravikant

This final section focuses on how you might apply the information and insight you've gained. This step starts with a simple question. *If you make no changes, how do you envision your company's future?*

Do you see growth? Expansion? Celebrating another year of increased sales? It's possible that you're feeling quite good about your direction, and this book has confirmed your decisions.

On the other hand, you may want to dig deeper into the challenges you face. You might be struggling with some level of uncertainty about the future. You may look down the road and see stagnation, financial stress, or a lack of vitality and direction.

You could have hit a plateau and, no matter what you do, you can't seem to recapture the exciting upward growth the company enjoyed at the beginning. Granted, this plateau could be a temporary slump, but what if it's the beginning of a decline you can't stop?

Maybe you're awake at night worrying about payroll. Is morale among your staff going down, and are you concerned that you might lose a key employee, or more? You could be upset about a rash of customer complaints or bad online reviews. How can you bolster the company's reputation now? Are investors losing interest as your bank balance decreases?

Let's face it: There are so many business challenges that you might even question if your dream is still worth pursuing. You may ask yourself, "Is this what I want to keep doing? Are the sacrifices I'm making worth the possible rewards?"

I've observed something very interesting while working with successful founders who dream of a company that profoundly impacts their industries. In the beginning, they are willing to take enormous risks. Look at the sacrifices founders make to start from scratch—some quit their day jobs, risking reliable income. Others set up offices in their dining rooms or work out of their garages at night. Even Builders, who are significantly risk-adverse, take a chance and bet on something new. With a dream, a passion, a conviction that they can make a difference, founders go all in, willing to work twenty-four seven to build their companies.

But once the startup experiences a measure of success, the founders become more cautious. Now that they have something tangible—people who are invested, customers who are buying, something they could lose—there can be a dramatic shift in outlook. That original "let's throw caution to the wind" attitude wanes. This is when their companies need founders to provide strong, clear, and effective leadership. The moment when a company needs to GrowUp is not the best time for founders to lose their mojo.

Incontrovertibly, this is the very moment your confidence in yourself and your company needs to be at its most robust. You will need to change to move into the next phase of success. Every successful leader knows that growth requires change.

Change Isn't Always Comfortable

Very few of us like change. Not really. We might not want to be bored or stagnant, but that doesn't mean we relish the discomfort, confusion, and newness that change demands. All change is, to some extent, inherently uncomfortable. Small changes might be annoying, but the level of change I'm suggesting might cause some pain.

So, at this juncture, it may appear more comfortable to avoid making a decision. Sure, you were brave when you started putting this whole thing together. But back then, you had less to lose. Now, you have employees who depend on you for their jobs. And customers who rely on your products and services. Everyone could lose if you make the "wrong" choice. It might feel more comfortable to wait a little longer before you decide.

However, deciding not to change is still a choice. If you choose to make no changes and continue to run your company the way you have, your businesses trajectory will continue in the same direction. Be honest with yourself about the risks of acting or not acting. Are you willing to risk what will happen if you continue as you have? Do you think it's safer to remain a startup rather than become a sustainable, growing company?

Here is the bottom line: If you want your company to Grow-Up, you must make changes. Period. And not just little ones. I mean *significant changes*. A few tweaks won't cut it.

I don't mean to scare or talk you out of expanding your company. I want to help you be clear on how motivated you are to become a different kind of leader—one capable of successfully transforming your startup into a thriving and sustainable company. I'm preparing you for what is to come so that you persevere and succeed.

If you want a different and better outcome, it's important to recognize that nothing will change if *you* don't make changes. Your company will not GrowUp without change, which starts with you and your choices. Undoubtedly, these changes will be pretty challenging.

1. Your Company is a Reflection of Who You Are

Keep in mind that founders naturally create startups in their own images, reflecting their values, strengths, and passions. It also means the founder's weaknesses and blind spots are present across the company. A friend of mine, Malte Kramer, the CEO of Luxury Presence, had an epiphany when I told him about the GrowUp framework over lunch. He said, "It makes sense. My team and I just analyzed the company's strengths and weaknesses. Looking at the list, I realized we'd identified my strengths and weaknesses. It was a bit startling."

Owning the fact that the company you've created embodies your abilities and shortcomings can make a founder feel vulnerable. It might even cause you some embarrassment. It can be unpleasant and even offensive to confront what isn't working in your startup because it can feel like you are failing somehow. It is very personal.

But now is not the time to lose confidence. The challenge is to stay nimble and take risks, not pull back and get defensive. When you first started, you stepped outside your comfort zone on a personal, relational, and organizational level. It's time to engage that attitude during the GrowUp phase as well.

Your company can only change and grow if you are taking the lead in that process. While your strengths are still needed, you won't be able to rely solely on yours like you did in the past. The answers won't come as naturally as they did at the beginning. The next strategy might require taking advice from those who have core competencies that you lack. Let's be honest here; change is hard for all of us. It can be especially difficult for someone like you, a strong leader accustomed to making most, if not all, of the decisions.

The biggest challenge in front of you right now is acknowledging that you, as the founder, are the creator of the most significant problems your company faces. Recognizing one's weak spots, especially in a leadership position, is not for the weak at heart. You may feel sad, a bit discouraged, and full of guilt over this newfound knowledge. Do not take it personally. Every business leader has blind spots to overcome—even the best leaders in the world. That is what makes them great leaders. They identify their weak spots and take them on as challenges, not limitations. You must do the same.

2. Embrace Your Blind Spot

I've seen it time and again. I work with a founder and we establish a good working relationship. All is going well until I suggest that the founder make one specific change. Suddenly, the atmosphere of the room seems to change.

Phrases like, "Don't be ridiculous," "That's completely unnecessary," and, "That would ruin my company," are flung across the room. I can sense a complete rejection of my recommendation. This isn't simply a difference of opinion. No, it's more than that. I've said something offensive. Even something personal. The respect my client has for me dissolves into thin air. Instantly, I go from trusted guide to someone who is a threat.

I used to be upset in these moments. But not anymore because that's when I recognize that we have just moved into the founder's blind spot. And it's never pretty.

The case has been made throughout this book that a company must have all four Superpowers represented and active for a startup to GrowUp. At first look, that might not seem so difficult. Translated into business jargon, that means a company needs to have a strong product-market fit (Innovator), a competent business operation (Builder), an articulated brand and a positive culture so that employees and customers alike are loyal (Connector), and a successful sales operation that convinces customers to buy (Persuader). It seems like common sense.

And yet it's not common for all of these areas to work in harmony with each other. That is especially the case when a startup is transitioning into a sustainable operation. Why? Because at least one of the G-R-O-W competencies or Superpowers is in the founder's blind spot.

I've worked with Innovators who expressed loathing for my suggestion to hire a Builder. "I won't let anyone tell me that I need to fill out some silly form or be told I can't spend money on what I think is important!"

Builders might have the same repulsion to Persuaders. "I don't want to bring in a salesperson who won't follow protocol! I can do the selling myself!"

Connectors can be appalled at an Innovator who offers ideas for new products. "Who gave this person the right to come up with these ideas? Everything has to go through me!"

Persuaders may roll their eyes at Connectors, and refuse to fund booths at industry conferences. I believe the founder's blind spot is the primary reason that startups fail. This means that you, the founder, must make this your first priority in your strategy for change.

How Can You Recognize Your Blind Spots?

You need to identify your blind spots and then acknowledge that your blind spots are your company's blind spots too. But here's the real rub. You can't see your blind spots, so identifying how they show up across your company will be difficult, if not impossible, on your own. That's why they are called blind spots.

Don't get me wrong, founders can identify many challenges their companies face. But there are key stumbling blocks to your success that you overlook. If it's any consolation, everyone does this. It's part of being human, I suppose.

While you don't see your own blind spots, others might. Most likely, a lot of people see them clearly. Perhaps they wish they could talk to you about them. Possibly, your employees, consultants, and friends have even tried. Only if founders are willing to listen and tolerate what feels like criticism will they likely discount what they're being told. They'll reject the advice or say it's somewhat accurate but not a priority at this time.

If you take some time to reflect, you might recall a situation when you've had such a conversation—someone pointing out a problem they see or a new direction for the team to go. As you re-member these moments, reflect on how you handled the situation. Did you embrace their views or dismiss their ideas as inaccurate or unimportant? Did you feel criticized and a bit defensive? One of the signs that someone has pointed out your blind spot is a negative emotional response. That's a tip-off that you can't see the problem, and it's outside your comfort zone.

Blind spots are hidden behind two closed doors: "It's not real," and "It's not important." If you refuse to open these doors when they appear, your company could very likely close its doors perma-nently. Being aware of yourself, your strengths, weaknesses, and blind spots are the first step in the ongoing process of scaling your company.

Foster awareness by creating a company culture where it's safe for your team to share their perspectives and creativity. Even Connectors who value culture and relational harmony will struggle to stay open to feedback for fear of tarnishing their reputation. No matter what your Superpower might be, it's critical that people are allowed to share their insights openly and ongoingly. No matter how well you tackle your blind spots right now, it is an ongoing effort to keep them at bay. They will always try to creep back into the equation as your company grows.

We all have blind spots, and it's very difficult for us to recognize our own. But the survival of your company is threatened by your lack of self-awareness, so dealing with this issue is truly a priority. Here are some suggestions to help you see what you normally don't see.

1. Ask people you trust

While you're unaware, it's possible, even plausible, that your friends and family know this part of your personality. It's even more likely that those who work with you, especially those who embody the Superpower or GROW competency that you unconsciously disdain, know this dark place exists. Your employees may have had negative interactions with you when they accidentally stepped into the blind zone.

It may be hard for you to accept that you would ever be rude to someone who works for you, and perhaps you never have. But you have probably shot down an idea during a brainstorming session with more intensity than you realized or you've made a joke at the expense of someone that triggers your blind spot.

2. Observe Yourself and Your Spontaneous Reactions

When we are triggered (and at some point in life we are), our reaction to the situation far outweighs the current situation. In other words, watch for when you over-react.

Did you get overly offended by something that was said? Have you felt more animosity towards someone than merited? People might have actually said to you, "You're over-reacting here." It's most likely a trigger for your blind spot.

3. Look at the areas of your company that are least developed.

If you are unaware of your blind spots, you will naturally fill all of your open positions with people like you. And you will never find the "right" person for that job because they are hiding in your blind spot. Even if you fill that position with the right Superpower, you will be inclined to unwittingly block them from doing their job or you may dislike them.

It is a complex fix. Look at the areas in your company that are least developed, even though you don't think it is remotely important. Be aware of your own reactions to people, their suggestions, and what they value. If it's in your blind spot, you might be unusually dismissive, sarcastic, critical, closed minded, or even enraged.

CHAPTER 14

Awareness, Assessment, and Adjustment

"The first step toward change is awareness.
The second step is acceptance."
—Nathaniel Branden

You've built a company that has experienced initial success, and that's something that no one can deny. When you first started, you knew, at least intellectually, that failing was an option. But you took the risk anyway, and off you went, pulling together people who believed in your dream and setting up ways to produce your products or deliver your services. You set up bank accounts and created a brand and, most likely, a website. And somehow, you raised enough funding from investors, friends, and family. So, you are successful at starting companies. Now you must decide your next step.

If you refuse to give up and are prepared to be unflinchingly honest with yourself and your leadership team, you have what it takes to turn things around. I won't sugarcoat it. The level of change this book suggests is hard—you may need to change your mind, behavior, perspective, and goals. And change is uncomfortable.

The question facing you right now is this: What changes do I need to make to ensure that all four Superpowers are present and active in my company? When is the right time to make these changes? Do I do them all at once or focus on the areas I need most right now?

To answer these questions, you have to apply everything you have learned in this book about the GrowUp model. Nothing is impossible. It just requires perseverance and a willingness to make change. So, if you want to be part of the ten percent of companies that survive, you need the right team and G-R-O-W competencies to stay in the game throughout the journey. And that is literally what the GrowUp model is—it's a journey. It is not a method applied once, and everything is clear sailing after that. No, it's not a once and for all process. Rather, it's a cycle that includes Awareness, Assessment, and Adjustment.

Phase One:
Awareness of Your Company

Now that you are aware of your own strengths, weaknesses, and blind spots, it is time to turn your attention to your company at large. As mentioned previously, your company is often a mirror of you. Your strengths are typically your *company's* strengths. Your weaknesses and blind spots are often the *company's* weaknesses and blind spots. Who you are as a founder informs not just what your company focuses on or doesn't but also who you have hired and not hired along the way. Let's a look at how this potentially plays out for each Superpower.

The Innovator's Company:
Speed Over Process

The Innovator creates a company with a super-clear vision and has employees who deliver new products and services against that vision faster than their competitors (Strength). However, as smaller customer requests start to pile up, no one is prioritizing them (Weakness), so they get some improvements done to quiet the loudest voice in the room, but not necessarily the most important ones. The list gets bigger and bigger while the team continues to play whack-a-mole. For example, suppose someone steps up to help with the prioritization effort (Builder). The company will reject the process and find workarounds to continue development on things that weren't deemed top priority (Company Blind Spot).

The Builder's Company:
Safety Over Risk

The Builder's company has a detailed plan against which they are executing at every organizational level. Everyone has clear goals and can connect their work to the company's success (Strength). Every decision the company makes is analyzed in painstaking detail, often leading to delay or no decision (Weakness). That can play out in various ways. For example, if someone has an idea that has never been done before (Innovator), the company rejects it as too risky (Blind Spot).

The Connector's Company:
Control Over Empowerment

Connectors care deeply about people and their collective team's reputation in the industry. A Connector's company is one with great relationships amongst peers and a stellar culture to go along with it (Strength). People understand that what they say and how they say it is of utmost importance, so they aren't always as direct with each other and their customers as they should be (Weakness). However, it can be problematic if someone tries to react quickly to an issue at hand. Others can speedily reprimand them if it goes sideways (Persuader). But the Connector prioritizes control over empowerment, so if someone tries something new without the proper approvals and it backfires, the team at large will look down on that person for going rogue (Blind Spot).

The Persuader's Company:
Customers Over Consistency

The Persuader creates a company that gets things done. The Persuader's team has perfected the art of the sale— whether that is signing customers, negotiating vendor contracts, or getting people internally to see their point of view (Strength). People do whatever it takes to accomplish their goals, which may impact the company's reputation from time to time (Weakness). So, if someone tries to reject a new customer's one-off request because it may impact how existing customers feel (Connector), they are instantly met with resistance. The team will not understand why they wouldn't give the customer exactly what they wanted.

Now that you are hyper aware of who you are as a founder, it should be significantly easier to see these characteristics within your company, especially the company's blind spot. Once you see it and can connect the dots between your blind spot and the company's blind spot, it will hit you like a ton of bricks in your daily interactions. It will feel as if someone took your rose-colored glasses off, and now you see the world clearly. I recognize that this can be confronting. You may have days where you are downright exhausted by the sheer number of times you see your blind spot in situations throughout your day. You are now in the eye of the storm, and the only way through it is change. The best way to avoid the emotional roller coaster is to proactively assess the situation and use the GrowUp model to plan your next steps.

Phase Two: Assessment

Even though founders often structure their companies around their core competencies, some activities may support the other competencies. However, without the founder intentionally including all four competencies, these efforts won't occur at the level you need them to scale.

As discussed in the previous section, this may be due to your blind spots as a founder. For example, if you are an Innovator, you have gained full conviction for your business model. You may be ramping up, albeit too slowly, due to your adverse reaction to process. While your reputation may be positive, it still requires more focus. Yes, you have won some customers, but you need more to move beyond a startup level. It is now time to take the next step and master the other three core competencies required to GrowUp successfully.

The most common reason for this lack of mastery is that the people you have dedicated to each competency need to have the right Superpowers for it to be prosperous. Yes they can do the job, but not as efficiently as someone with those core competency skills. For instance, you may have someone other than a Builder focused on policies and procedures. A clue to this mismatch would be finding parts of the process the person you've placed in charge has not thought through in detail or have even forgotten. Another telltale sign is how much satisfaction a person experiences in a specific role. A Builder will enjoy building, but an Innovator, Connector, or Persuader will not. A mismatched team member doesn't receive the natural rewards our brains give us when we are freed to do what we do best. You'll get the best results when the job and the Superpower match.

Founder	G-R-O-W Competency (Pro)	Blind Spot (Con)
Innovator	Gain Conviction	Process
Builder	Ramp Up	Risk-Taking
Connector	Own Your Reputation	Empowerment
Persuader	Win Customers	Consistency

The only way to truly know this is to have each leadership team member take the Superpower Test from Chapter 1. This test is also available online at michelledenogean.com. I encourage you to have everyone on your team take the test and send you the results.

Plug the results in below:
You might be surprised at what this exercise reveals.

Employee Name	Employee Superpower	Current Job Title	Core Competency Required for job	Superpower Needed to Master Core Competency	Do the Super-powers Match?
					Y / N
					Y / N
					Y / N

Reflections:
- Does your team represent all four Superpowers? If not, which ones are missing?
- Are your team members in job positions that match their Superpowers? If not, how would you set up the organization differently with this knowledge?
- Is there someone on your team whose Superpower sits squarely in your blind spot? How has your behavior gotten in the way of their ability to be successful?

Now that you have reflected deeply on your current situation, it is time to implement these insights. If you find that many people on your team share the same Superpower as you, don't worry. This is very common. People are naturally attracted to people like themselves. It isn't necessarily bad, but it does mean you are over-indexed on your core competency and need to become more balanced as a leadership team. Lacking the other three Superpowers will be detrimental to your success in the long run. So, what does a founder do? Will you let go of these amazing individuals who likely helped you start the company, or move them around and supplement what is lacking?

The next steps may seem obvious, but they can be quite confronting. Don't panic. Successful founders before you have been through this and come out the other side. There are many solutions to this problem that won't impact your company's culture or break the bank. Let's get into it.

Phase Three: Adjustments

Now that you know which Superpowers are missing from your organization requiring you to add people, and which Superpowers you have in place but need to empower further based on your blind spots, it is time to take action. Often, this involves moving people around in the organization so that they can do what they do best

I recommend you talk with your leaders individually or as a team about the results to assess your company's current reality accurately. You may think one thing is the case, but those working with you see the situation from a completely different perspective. It might be challenging for you personally or as a leader, but I can't stress this enough. Discussion needs to occur in order to make the changes necessary to GrowUp.

Consideration 1: Can you reorganize who you already have to fill in the four core competencies?

It is possible that you have precisely what you need to master the G-R-O-W competencies required, but you may not have everyone in the right seat.

Someone lower in the organization often has the Superpower necessary to fulfill the missing competency and could be moved into your leadership team. You may need to go a few layers down in the organization and have those people take the Superpower test to identify if this is the case. A promotion might be in order in the person is ready for leadership. If you see this person as needing more experience or training, keeping them where they are might be best. However, you must empower each of your employees to do what they do best. It is critical to do so. Moving people to the right spot now could be essential to long-term survival.

If you already have a well-balanced team across the organization but scored lower than you would like on one or more G-R-O-W competencies, it is time to play some musical chairs. Regardless of person's current title, put them in charge of the core competency they are aligned with. If this feels like an overwhelming task, given current roles and responsibilities, it is okay to take baby steps.

Consider making them a sponsor of that core competency—someone who leads that function without managing it directly for ninety days—and then evaluate them to determine your next step. Given your blind spots, you may have a hard time envisioning a particular individual leading a specific effort, so a ninety-day trial may be what you need to see what is possible. If this person is lower in the organization, make sure your entire leadership team is aware of their blind spots for this individual to succeed.

If your evaluation indicates that the person isn't a good fit, it may be time to look outside the building for that talent. You will need to decide if this is a replacement role or an additive role depending on where your company is in its growth trajectory.

Well done if you marked yourself low on a particular competency and have an employee focused in that area with the associated Superpower. Now, it is time to empower them. Unfortunately, this is easier said than done. Blind spots often get in the way. Consider these concerns:

- Innovators hate process because they want to move at lightning speed. As a result, Innovators can sabotage Builders by working around their process to get things done.
- On the flip side, Builders are naturally analytical and, therefore, have a hard time with Innovators who take enormous risks that are not guaranteed. As a result, Builders may sabotage the Innovator by asking for proof before they proceed.
- Connectors care deeply about every detail that could impact the company's reputation and, as a result, may stop a Persuader from experimenting to get deals done.
- Because Persuaders prioritize closing the deal, they are likely to ignore the Connector's concern for protecting the company's reputation.

Consider talking to people you trust outside your organization who embody your opposite Superpower to gain perspective. It can be challenging to recognize what you naturally choose to ignore. Bring them on as a coach to help keep your awareness high. But don't underestimate the significance of self-awareness and the potential to hold people back from mastering what you genuinely need them to do.

With a keen awareness of your behavior, the best course of action is to stay out of your team's way and let them do what they do best. Use this book as a reminder of your team's core competencies and their importance in your quest to GrowUp.

Consideration 2: Is it time to supplement your team with people who hold missing Superpowers?

Once you have assessed your organization and the possibility of moving people around, you may need to add a few people to master all four G-R-O-W competencies. It may be tempting to bring in all the people you are missing immediately. However, the way to go is to pick the competency with the lowest score and find one employee, consultant, or advisor with this Superpower. Why is this important?

If you bring in multiple people at once, especially when that area has been neglected, the organization could be overwhelmed by the speed of change required. Adding new staff is always disruptive to a certain degree, but this kind of change will alter the company's inner workings. That will be a lot for you and your team to deal with.

Be aware that even if you have the budget to hire someone full-time, hiring may not be the best action in the near term. After all, there is a reason why you haven't thought that core competency was crucial until now. It has been in your blind spot, so there are elements to this transition that you have yet to consider.

I recommend that you talk to some seasoned individuals in your network about the gap or find an experienced consultant and get advice on what you need. It's essential to seek the guidance of individuals who hold the missing Superpower. These conversations will help you anticipate and avoid landmines buried beneath your awareness. You'll be better able to make changes that your company experiences as wins rather than a source of conflict.

From the insights, mistakes, and learning gained from this measured first step, you and your team will gain further clarity around the type and number of people you need to hire to GrowUp successfully in the near future.

Remember, this will challenge you personally. If you can stay present to your blind spots, with an open mind rather than becoming defensive, you can have an extremely rewarding experience. Be prepared that you may have strong negative reactions to your own decisions. These opposing Superpowers have likely been foreign to you up until now, so you'll need to learn new ways to lead your team. But the chances for success will grow as you chart new territory.

The goal is to discover the winning strategy that exponentially grows your company. Even mistakes will reveal what your next step ought to be. So when you hit a few bumps on the way, even big ones, accept this is a normal part for the GrowUp journey.

Consideration 3: What is the best time to bring on new people?

Hiring is a bit like Goldilocks seeing three bowls of porridge—one is too hot, one is too cold, so she settles in with the third option, which is just right. There could be no better analogy for what happens in the startup world when it comes to staffing. Making timely decisions is everything. Having been on both sides of this equation—hiring too slow and too fast—I will say they are equally dangerous.

Who you are as a founder will play a big role in the speed at which you hire. Persuaders and Builders tend to

> **Having been on both sides of this equation—hiring too slow and too fast—I will say they are equally as dangerous.**

more analytical and hire slowly, while Connectors and Innovators see the big picture and want to go fast. Regardless of the type of founder you are, I strongly encourage you to go slow at first to make sure you have leaders who can develop each of the four G-R-O-W competencies within the organization. Take time for each to get established before expanding the teams underneath them. Only then should you focus on how fast or slow you can grow to support those competencies.

Hiring Too Fast

Companies that are able to hire immediately are those who have the funds available. Congratulations if you have raised a lot of money upfront. That is a huge accomplishment!

But the watch-out for you is hiring too quickly. If you have a lot of money in the bank, it is easy to spend. I have seen this repeatedly with startups, especially those who raised venture capital funds and are now in later-stage fundraising rounds. That amount of money does funny things to people. Partly due to pressure from the board of directors to grow at an astronomical rate—which is real—and partly due to the sigh of relief people get when they have that level of funding.

Either way, money leads to spending, and you will spent too much if you aren't careful. Some of it will be on unimportant things like parties or extravagant office space, but it is often spent with the best intention of hiring people.

The funny thing about teams is that they always feel like they need more resources. People have a way of keeping more than busy, especially if they aren't laser-focused. So, when you raise a lot of money, everyone comes to the table with resource needs. It is easy to see how it happens. Five people in finance, ten people in product, twenty people in sales, fifteen in support, two or three in marketing, three in recruiting to help hire these people, five in HR to support the new hires, and so on.

Be mindful that even if you need all of those people, hiring more than an additional twenty percent of your employee base all at once will be impossible for you to digest as a company. Productivity will slow down rather than speed up as you ask existing employees to train new employees, and people without any management experience are expected to take on direct reports. Consider growing in phases, focusing on the most prominent parts of the business first and giving yourself time and grace for those new employees to get settled in. Your long-term success will thank you for it.

Hiring Too Slowly

Most founders will worry that they don't have the means to hire everyone they need quickly because they are trying to stretch every dollar. If you are overly cautious about hiring, you may not only burn out your existing employees to the point of departure, but you also risk falling behind your competitors by not stoking the flame to stay ahead of them. If not managed correctly, failure to hire will have big cultural impacts on the people who remain at the company, leaving you with critical roles to backfill and the ones you need to add into the mix working elsewhere.

You may think, well, that's okay. The areas where we need staffing aren't mission-critical, but I urge you to reconsider that line of thinking. Burnout spreads like wildfire through a company. When the team that wasn't mission-critical loses a few people, it impacts adjacent groups that worked alongside those resources. Your company is something like a jigsaw puzzle—removing one piece could dismantle your productivity overall.

If you find yourself in a more budget-conscious situation, it's imperative to find creative ways to keep burnout at bay. It comes down to a simple "triangle of objectives." The triangle of objectives was a term coined by Dr. Martin Barnes in the 1980s. (stakeholdermap.com, Project Management Triangle, Tam M, 2021)

The three points of the triangle represent quality, cost, and time. The idea here is that one of these three points is always fixed, making the other two points move in one direction or the other. So, if cost is constrained, quality and time are adjusted to compensate.

All of this is fancy speak to say that if you can't hire more people, you will need to prioritize so that you don't lose your existing employees to burnout. This is easier said than done when competitive pressures are underway. However, there are always creative ways to ensure you stay ahead of the curve. Part-time consultants may be a solution depending on the role, or it may just be going all in on one area that will truly set you apart. It is surmountable, but it does take strategic focus.

Consideration 4: How will you best integrate new hires into the existing team?

Your company already has a culture in place, whether you have invested in that intentionally or not. The people on your team are part of a group that knows and shares your dreams and aspirations. They also know you and what makes you tick, what to say and what not to say. And, whether it's formalized or not, your team has a pecking order, and everyone knows it. They have a way of using their power to achieve their goals and objectives. And while the team may think they want more people to help with tasks to avoid burnout, it's always an adjustment when new people arrive. The entire group order is changed.

That is why it is important to hire for cultural fit. It's as important as hiring to fill a G-R-O-W competency you lack. If you hire someone who excels at a core competency but does not share the same values as the rest of your team, they will not work out in the end. The existing team will reject them, making it impossible for them to succeed. Employees who share the same values get

> **Your company already has a culture in place, whether you have invested in that intentionally or not.**

along from the get-go and easily integrate quickly. People accept working with people they like, and sharing personal values is the key to making this happen.

It is important to acknowledge that you can have a team with all four Superpowers that share the same values. The strengths that an individual holds to get the job done are not the same qualities that make them a good teammate. Your company values are what define how you show up to one another. If one of your values is Care, it is possible to hire a Builder to implement process and analyze data who cares deeply about the people they work with. They may stop you from hiring more people, but they will care deeply about the people you have. If transparency is one of your values, it is possible to hire a Connector whose personal reputation is all about being transparent. They may care deeply about the company's reputation, but it's possible that transparency is part of the reputation they produce.

In addition to cultural fit, make sure that everyone at the company understands how their role might change with this new person in place. Everyone needs to understand their own Superpower and associated strengths, what is being asked of them from a focus perspective, and how this new individual will compliment versus completely replace them. If you can remove any element of threat from the equation and show your appreciation for what the existing team brings to the table, integration will go smoothly.

Reflections:
- Can you re-organize who you already have on staff, regardless of their level, to fill in the four G-R-O-W competencies? What would your organizational chart look like if you did?
- Do you need to supplement your team with people who hold certain Superpowers? If yes, which G-R-O-W competency do you need the most?
- Do you know anyone in your network that can act as an advisor/mentor in the meantime? Do they align with your company's culture?

CHAPTER 15

When Do You Need to Pivot?

"A pivot is a change in strategy without a change in vision".
–Eric Ries

As you bring all four Superpowers into the mix, you will quickly discover that you need to make changes to GrowUp your business. Many of these will be simple adjustments that we discussed in the last chapter. You might implement a new process, modify your brand positioning in the market, or hire new people. These are all relatively easy changes, especially if you stay aware of your blind spots and bring in people who have mastered the G-R-O-W competencies to adjust accordingly.

However, sometimes the changes necessary are much bigger and require you to completely change the direction of your business. This can mean developing a completely new product or service or finding a totally new target audience because what you have built isn't meeting the needs of your current customers. These business model changes are called pivots. They are sharp left turns you were not expecting to make but are necessary for survival.

Pivots are intense, as they often bring up those feelings of failure. Knowing that your business will not survive without drastic change can be devastating. To many, it means that their original vision was flawed. And as the founder, this can be very personal for you. Openly admitting that your baby will not GrowUp in its current incarnation can be quite depressing.

I am here to tell you that there is nothing wrong with having to pivot. Some of the most successful companies of all time were completely different companies before they hit it big. In this chapter we will talk about companies like YouTube, Play-Doh and Slack to name a few.

Having seen several pivots first-hand, I am here to tell you they

> "
> There is nothing wrong with having to pivot. Some of the most successful companies of all time were completely different companies before they hit it big.

can reinvigorate you and your team if you confidently lead them through it. Why? Because once you realize what needs to be done, and the path forward is clear, the new focus will excite people. The incredible team you have built around you, will swarm the problem and come out the other side as a strong, more close-knit family having almost crashed the plane and then survived.

Developing Your Pivot Strategy

You need all four Superpowers to not only identify the need for a pivot but also develop the go-forward business plan. It is natural to want to identify these things before you expand your payroll.

Advisors or consultants may be a good interim choice to help you evaluate your next step. Find people in your network with the missing Superpowers needed to assess your business and ask them for their support. Invite them to examine your business from all angles. While they may not be able to solve the problems they see, they will ask the questions you need to identify areas of weakness and potential opportunity.

Each superpower will most likely see deficits that are in their area of strength. For example, an Innovator will be adept at assessing whether or not you have product-market fit. If you bring on a Connector, you may find that your reputation has taken a beating. Builders may point out the lack of effective procedures, and Persuaders will see what needs to be improved for increasing sales.

But there is one problem that is significant enough to cause a company to pivot—the lack of product-market fit. In simple terms, it means that you are trying to sell a product to a customer base that doesn't feel the need for it.

If you discover this is accurate, let me give you some straightforward advice: Don't panic! Some of the most successful companies in the world today have made major pivots, which is precisely why they are the most successful. Let's look at how this can be done.

We will address two flavors of business pivots in this chapter.

1. Pivoting to an adjacent problem for your existing target audience
2. Pivoting to an adjacent audience for your existing products

Pivoting to an Adjacent Problem

If you are deeply invested in a specific target audience, pivoting to an adjacent problem is the simpler option. In many cases, it doesn't mean giving up your original vision. The pivot could be an additive until you feel out the marketplace to understand the opportunity's size.

To pivot to an adjacent problem, I recommend that you interview a large number of your current customers. Dig deep into their daily lives and identify all the issues they experience. Discover which ones would have the most significant impact if you solved them.

YouTube is an excellent example of this. When the company started in 2005, it was a video dating website that allowed people to share short videos describing their ideal partner. With online dating websites fully established by the mid-2000s, YouTube's video dating idea was a bit of a flop. They couldn't even pay women to post videos there. (The Guardian, Dredge, 2016)

But YouTube as we know it today is a successful video streaming service primarily targeting men and women between the ages of twenty-five and thirty-four. It's the same target audience but solving very different problems.

They discovered that same demographic wanted to upload videos about many other subjects to the web. Hence, they pivoted the company, broadening the offering to the same target audience. Today, YouTube generates over thirty billion dollars in advertising revenue. They have come a long way since their video dating website days.

Pivoting to an Entirely New Target Audience

The second choice, pivoting to a whole new target audience, is more challenging but doable. After all, you have invested in understanding a particular target audience, have built a reputation, and may have some paying customers.

It's critical to get out and talk to people to understand if there is a different audience for your product or service. Start by ideating about the various applications of what you have built. Speak with people who you believe would apply the product in that way. What problems do they have? Is your product or service something that would solve that problem for them? Would it have a significant impact?

Often, a new target audience is discovered by accident. You could be looking in one direction and discover a subgroup or a completely different type of customer that fits perfectly.

I caution you, however, to do further research before running full force toward that new audience. Make sure you put the same rigor into interviewing potential customers to ensure that there is enough of a target audience to feel confident you have product-market fit. Do not despair—take time to assemble a solid strategy before making any rash decisions. It is important to understand that pivots don't happen instantly. They tend to happen slowly and in concert with the existing business, where the new idea and audience are added before discontinuing the old.

One of the most iconic examples of this type of pivot comes from Play-Doh. Play-Doh was founded in 1912 by company named Kutol. *Fortune Magazine* stated that Play-Doh's original intent was to be a wall cleaner targeting homemakers. (Fortune, Kell, 2016) The product was a success for a few decades until the transition from heating with coal to oil, gas, and electricity occurred in the 1930s. After that, sooty buildup on wallpaper was no longer an issue.

They were trying to turn around the struggling company when the founder's sister-in-law read an article about using wallpaper cleaner for modeling projects. Since she was a teacher, she brought it into the classroom, and the kids loved molding it into all sorts of shapes and sizes. The pivot quickly took hold.

Play-Doh has sold over three billion cans since its debut as a child's toy, eclipsing its previous existence as a wallpaper cleaner by light years. Same exact product, a completely different target audience. Talk about product-market fit! So, talk to some customers. I promise it will be an invaluable experience.

There is power in pivoting when you understand its purpose. The idea is to recognize the need as soon as possible and be prepared by continuously walking in your customer's shoes. No one wants to be caught off guard and find it's too late to make a change.

Please note this important point: Having an Innovator on your team will ensure you stay a step ahead. Innovators are masters at deciphering the type of pivot needed because they are natural problem solvers used to constant change. They incessantly speak with potential customers and can identify things like their target audience's problems shifting. Do they have new issues? What other products and services are they entertaining? Why? How are market dynamics impacting them? They are continuously sourcing answers to a lot of questions to stay current. It is hard to get product-market fit, but it is easy to lose it if you aren't paying attention.

If you are not an Innovator, pivoting is easier said than done. Depending on how far along you are building your business, it may feel like you are trying to turn the Titanic. But don't give up. Put your ego aside, no matter how confronting the idea of changing your business may be.

Don't become part of the ninety-percent of founders who close their doors. Needing to pivot is not failure. Failing is choosing to give up. A pivot can be a vital move to transform your small startup into a huge success.

> **Needing to pivot is not failure. Failure is choosing to give up.**

CHAPTER 16

The Importance of Not Giving Up

*"Success is not final; failure is not fatal:
it is the courage to continue that counts."*
—Winston Churchill

We have come full circle from the first chapter to the last, facing the walls all founders find looming in the road, obstructing their paths. One of the options a founder confronts along the way—and usually more than once—is the choice to quit.

If the obstacles seem too overwhelming and you decide to close the doors, you won't be alone in making that decision. As mentioned in this book, ninety percent of founders give up on their dream for one reason or another. Their companies may be known as notable startups or small ventures that no one recalls. Big or small, grand or modest, these founders decided to give up before their organizations could GrowUp. If you give up, your company will join that list. The reason I do the work I do as a business consultant and why I wrote this book is to encourage you *not to give up.*

Millions of founders have effectively transitioned from startups to GrowUp, and it's never easy. Even if it appears there is no way forward for your company, I believe there is still hope—but only if you embrace the reality that *growth requires change*. Hard work and changing course are challenging, but that option is open to you.

You have what you didn't have when you first started reading this book: new information, deeper personal insight, innovative strategies, and role models of those who have gone before you. Your company can become part of the ten percent if you continually increase your awareness, conduct assessments, adjust, and even pivot if needed. You could survive and become a leader in your industry. But it all rests on you. *Will you continue to invest in your company or close the doors?*

Companies Who Know How to GrowUp

I'd like to share some success stories of companies that faced serious setbacks and yet were able to make the necessary changes. A vital component of the GrowUp process is including and utilizing all four of the Superpowers in your company.

Slack, a platform to help businesses with communication and project management, is an excellent example of a company that achieved this goal. But they didn't start as a wild success. On the contrary, Slack was born from failure, according to Techcrunch. (The Slack Story Origin, Clark, 2019)

The founders of Slack started a gaming company called Tiny Speck and raised a bunch of money to launch their initial game—but it never took off. They couldn't attract a large enough audience. The problem was so severe that they made a massive audience and business model pivot.

They kept the internal collaboration tool their team built at Tiny Speck and made it available to the masses. Today, over 600,000 organizations around the world use Slack! Over ten million people use the platform daily to communicate and coordinate with their co-workers.

What I love about Slack is that they knew from the beginning that they had to focus on individual teams within companies, not the buyers. They purposely set out to create team experiences like no other company did then. They redefined a communication category. But making this transition can take some time.

They gained conviction by using the product as a company, inviting individuals they knew to use it for free during a "preview release," and letting word of mouth spread like wildfire. In a Product Board blog, Slack's chief product officer, Tamar Yehoshua, said, "Customer-centricity is a team sport. Everybody has to be focused on the customer. We get feedback from many places, but the key is putting yourself in the customers' shoes."

When it came to ramping up, Slack had no real trouble raising funds. By 2019, they had created a fun brand and obsessed over customer feedback to keep the product fresh.

Did they Own Their Reputation? Indeed they did! The Slack brand stands for teaming—being efficient—and, more importantly, creating personal connections with colleagues. By focusing on word of mouth and connecting teams on a personal level, they built a brand that people became passionate about. So, without a CMO, spending a dime on advertising, or a fancy creative agency, they created a fun, memorable brand that delivers a consistent experience that people talk about. It is reflected in their vibrant colors and fun logo design. Still, these are outputs of an internal focus and clarity of purpose that the founders set out to accomplish.

How did Slack win so many customers? By offering their base product for free. Anyone at any company could sign up for Slack with a small group of co-workers and use it until they couldn't live without it. Since Slack was built with teams in mind, they could expand one person at a time. They knew from experience using the tools themselves that getting usage up and running takes time.

Once they started charging a nominal fee, people were already hooked on using it to share information. It was affordable for managers to expense their Slack account to the company. They eventually hired a Chief Sales Officer in 2016 to expand their footprint into Enterprise sales. Still, this freemium model served them well in persuading customers. By 2021, Slack had scaled to thousands of employees and was approached for acquisition by Salesforce.com for $28 billion.

But let me point out that they could have given up when Tiny Speck failed so severely. Discouragement could have undermined their determination. Instead, they pulled together and created an entirely new company. They mastered the pivot, that's for sure!

On a much smaller scale, Roadster had a very similar trajectory. Andy Moss, CEO, is an Innovator. He started Roadster with four software engineers and designers he had previously worked with. With zero automotive experience, they chose that industry because it was one of the few big-ticket categories left where you still needed help to buy online. With passion and confidence based on their abilities, Andy and his co-founders set out to disrupt the automotive industry by enabling car purchases online. With a pivot or two, Roadster was one of the ten percent who were able to go from startup to GrowUp. As the company's CMO, I had a front-row seat.

Let's break down the Roadster story by the four GrowUp competencies and the people with Superpowers who made it happen.

Gain Conviction

Andy Moss, CEO and Innovator. Andy had the insight to purchase a car brokerage service early on to learn the ropes of selling cars online. When we pivoted the company to sell our software to dealerships nationwide, he spent hours with local dealerships in the San Francisco area, learning about their pain points and how we could innovate to solve their biggest problems.

Ramp Up

Rudi Thun, COO is part Connector and part Builder, alongside Builders Matt Wolf, CFO, and Lisa Macnew, VP of People. They were instrumental in the fundraising process, set the stage for the metrics that mattered, and formalized the plan related to people, systems, and other resources.

Own Your Reputation

Michelle Denogean, CMO—part Connector and part Innovator, alongside Rudi Thun, who helped keep our culture alive. I came in and built the brand from scratch, including the vast network of influencers who sang our praises. My deep understanding of the customer's mindset built a lot of our reputation. I wasn't completely aware of how different that was from other marketers until I started writing this book.

Win Customers

Amit Chandarana, SVP of Sales—fearless Persuader, our rainmaker who brought us relationships with the auto manufacturers and key dealer groups that were influential to the rest of the dealer body when it came to the products they bought.

Give Up or GrowUp?

You may be tempted to give up at several points in the GrowUp journey. Don't. In Barack Obama's words, "The real test is not whether you avoid this failure because you won't. It's whether you let it harden or shame you into inaction, or whether you learn from it; whether you choose to persevere."

As you can see in the Slack and Roadster examples, there were moments when each company could have easily given up. Instead, they pushed through and became wild successes in their own right. There are several points in the GrowUp journey where your conviction will waver. To get in front of those moments, let's spend a few minutes discussing each pressure point in the system and what to do when you get there.

There are times when founders feel like giving up. It's a feeling that is more common than you might think. So how can you know when to close the doors and when you just need to step back, take a deep breath, and try to new strategy?

I recommend that founders anticipate when they might be most tempted to give up. I've identified three times when founders feel extra stressed out. Let's start with the moment that you realize that your Superpower can't carry your company over the finish-line without some reorganization.

1. You may feel like giving up when you realize your company has only one Superpower

Since most founders rely solely on their Superpower, it can be quite upsetting to recognize that everyone they have hired shares the same strengths and weaknesses. This is a problem for future growth and must be addressed to GrowUp. But this realization doesn't have to mean that it's time to quit. Rather, it's the time to remember that this one Superpower made you great at starting your company. It is the Superpower that your company embodies, and that's a strong starting place.

Now is not the time to lose confidence or discard your vision. The company wouldn't exist without you and your phenomenal strengths. Take pride in your brilliance and what you have accomplished so far. That is an opportunity, not a limitation. You made your company great. You did that. And it will be you who finds incredible individuals with the other three Superpowers to realize your company's full potential.

M.G. Seigler, general partner at Google Ventures, quotes T.E. Lawrence in Lawrence of Arabia, "Big things have small beginnings." (Seigler, 500ish, 2015) In other words, the most accomplished companies may have had humble beginnings. It is easy for a startup founder to try and do everything all at once, especially when you hear something may not be going well in your business. Give yourself time to rectify this and celebrate that you get to do so.

When you think about it from a different perspective, this insight is an inspiring milestone. It is the decision point that will launch your company into its next growth phase. Push forward and be proud.

2. You may feel like giving up when you realize your blind spot is the reason you might fail

It can be embarrassing or at least humbling to own the fact that you have a blind spot inherent in your personality. But be aware, every founder around the globe has blind spots. Companies are run by humans (at least so far in our lifetime), and blind spots are part of human nature. We cannot know what we cannot see. You are reading this book and working to identify your blind spots, putting you light-years ahead of other companies like yours. You are on your way to being part of the ten percent.

When you identify your blind spot, you're no longer blind to it. It's out in the open; you can address it like any other challenge your business faces. That gives you an edge in making your company a success. Acknowledge your blind spots openly with your team and start taking action to bring on and empower the right people to master all four competencies. While you do this, be kind to yourself.

Covering up your failure for fear of being vulnerable will be tempting. However, the more vulnerable you can be as a leader, the more approachable you become, and as a result, the more dedicated your team will be. People like to feel needed and appreciated. Sharing areas of weakness allows your team to provide value. They will happily step up to the plate. Don't take that away from them. Let their Superpowers shine.

3. You may feel like giving up when you realize you might need to pivot your company

A pivot is, by its nature, a seismic shift in your business plan. It can feel like you've failed, and on one hand, you have to acknowledge that what you initially thought would work didn't turn out as expected. However, pivots are not failures; they are opportunities for success. Period. Pivots are brave. Yes, you have spent an enormous amount of time cultivating the company that you have built so far, but holding on to that concept in its current iteration could lead to the one thing you are trying to avoid at all costs—failure.

Take control of your narrative and make the pivot intentional and inspirational. According to Steve Jobs, "If you really look closely, most overnight successes took a long time." Playdough is a great example of this. They stumbled upon a new audience for their product when the founder's sister-in-law brought it into her classroom. What a great and memorable story. Your pivot can be the same. Lean into the aha moment that leads you to the pivot. It could be the story that makes your company famous.

With the proper framework, you can successfully go from startup to GrowUp. As my dear friend and now two-time colleague, Andy Moss, says, "Startups are a game of attrition. Winning is about perseverance, which requires one to stay in the game and weather whatever comes your way. There are a lot of twists and turns, but with the right team and G-R-O-W competencies in place, you will nail it when the right opportunity arises."

Don't give up. A founder with the right team in place will find its way, even if the company and the solutions offered look nothing like the original vision. It all starts with you. If you can recognize your Superpower, identify your personal blind spot and stay open to change—anything is possible. The saying, "What doesn't kill you makes you stronger," is authentic when it comes to going from startup to GrowUp.

My Story: When I Wanted to Give Up

We all have moments in our careers when the wall seems too thick, too high, too wide to overcome. This doesn't happen solely to founders. Let me share my story with you.

First, let me tell you that I am a Connector. This Superpower has served me well in my career as a marketing executive and business coach.

I have built incredible brands with clear purpose and reputations that people only dream of having. And now, after twenty-plus years in the seat, I am an incredible people leader too. Seriously. The teams that have worked for me have complimented my leadership style. Many of them have followed me from company to company. I worked hard to become a leader who empowers her team. It has taken concerted effort.

I had to fight the demons inside that want to control everything. Even before my first job, I knew I was a perfectionist. I had the best grades, cared deeply about what other people thought of me, and didn't take on anything I didn't feel like I could master. The younger me was all about my personal reputation, and I went into the workforce with this mindset front and center. Never let anyone see you fail.

And, I didn't fail for a very long time. I didn't fail until I did. And when I did fail, I failed hard. As I went from individual contributor to manager, this perfectionist tendency got the best of me. I believed that no one could do things as well as I could. I was sure it wouldn't turn out right if I delegated a task. Sure, my team had responsibilities, but they were rarely handed off anything of importance. I kept all of those projects for myself. To upper management, the team looked like rockstars, but to my team, I wasn't a leader at all.

I unwittingly set up a pattern. When we were assigned a project, I hoarded it for quite some time. I would kick it off, hear all the background, and hang onto it. Then, the next project came along, and I did the same thing. Eventually, my plate got so full that I was forced to hand something off—but rather than empowering my team, it felt like I was dumping a disaster onto someone else's lap. That feeling was accurate because I waited until the project was in trouble to get assistance. Do you know how that felt to my employees? Awful. They had zero ownership over what they were working on. They didn't understand the "why" behind their work. There was zero pride.

I had such a blind spot around Empowerment that it took members of the team complaining to HR for me to recognize it.

And when that uprising happened, it hit me like a ton of bricks. I couldn't understand it at first. I thought we were doing so well. How could this be? The truth is, with my hands tight on the steering wheel, my team didn't understand the strategy, they didn't feel like they owned a piece of it, and they didn't feel connected to me. I couldn't fathom this. I thought I had built strong relationships, knew their personal situations, and always asked about their weekends. How could they feel that way?

That moment in my career haunted me for a very long time. It would invade my dreams, waking me up in the middle of the night with horrible anxiety. I would keep my phone next to my bed to take notes as things I was doing wrong, people I hadn't recognized, or strategies that I had not fully explained came to my brain in the wee hours of the morning. In the middle of the night, my subconscious scanned the day for anything that had happened in the peripheral of my blind spot. Both my mental and physical health suffered as this perfectionist came to terms with what I had gone wrong.

All of this turmoil was emerging from my blind spot. Now, I was awakened. While I hadn't seen it for so many years, I suddenly saw it so clearly.

I could have let this stop me. I could have hung up my hat as a leader and gone back to being an individual contributor. Alternatively, I could have plowed ahead at different companies, doing my best to build relationships with the people I wouldn't let lead or fail. A lot of leaders like me have made it through their entire careers this way. But I decided that I was going to use this to become a better leader. I chose to change.

I learned to use my Superpower for good and set an inspiring vision that my team believed in. I brought in the entire team to discuss ways we could accomplish our goals. Together, we defined the parameters of the brand so everyone, not just me, could keep our reputation intact. The team thrived. They were challenged to come up with their own solutions and drive the implementation from start to finish.

Yes, errors happen occasionally, and I have to be okay with it. It was never easy; truthfully, it still isn't. I have learned to recognize when this dark side of my leadership capabilities rears its head and tell it to go away. I make the effort to let others flourish in recognition of their growth.

Most importantly, I have come to appreciate the other Superpowers on my team. As a Connector, I don't need a team of uniformed Connectors. In fact, we would not accomplish our goals if we were all that way. The Builder is a great compliment to my visionary ways. They make sure it all gets done on time. The Innovators bring great ideas that I would never have thought of on alone. And the Persuaders grow the business. Sure, they don't follow the rules, but we have learned to respect one another. When they start to veer off path with their positioning, I strive to understand why so that we can get them back on track.

Was it easy? Oh, no. Was it worth it? Absolutely.

Don't worry if you aren't exactly where you want to be. Don't be stopped. I kept going after a very public failure, and look at what happened. A breakthrough is possible. It can lead you to places you never thought possible. Use the tools in this book to guide you through the journey.

It's not too late to take your company to the next level. The world is your oyster once you know what it takes and who you need to make it happen. Go get it!

Reflections of
THE INNOVATOR

Are you an Innovator?

- In what ways do you exhibit the traits of an Innovator?
- What qualities of the Innovator do you wish to develop?
- Are there elements of the Innovator that feel completely foreign?

Gain Conviction: The Superpower of Innovation

- Does someone in your company have the Superpower of Innovation?
- Do any of the mistakes made by other Superpowers resonate with you?

Overcoming the Innovator's Blind Spot: Process

- Do you or someone on your team have a blind spot related to process?
- How has this blind spot shaped the relationships within your company?
- Can you think of times when you or someone else on your team reacted poorly to process?
- Is there someone in your company being sabotaged for putting process in place?
- What would happen if they were empowered to implement process?
- How often do you have difficulty planning ahead?
- How often do you get lost in the vision?
- How often do you prioritize your ideas over others?

NOTES

_____

_____

_____

_____

_____

_____

_____

_____

_____

_____

_____

Reflections of
THE BUILDER

Are you a Builder?

- In what ways do you exhibit the traits of a Builder?
- What qualities of the Builder do you wish to develop?
- Are there elements of the Builder that feel completely foreign?

Ramp Up: The Superpower of Building

- Does someone in your company have the Superpower to Build?
- Do any of the mistakes made by other Superpowers resonate with you?

Overcoming the Builder's Blind Spot: Risk Taking

- Do you or a team member have a blind spot related to risk taking?
- How has this blind spot shaped the relationships within your company?
- Can you think of times when you or someone on your team reacted poorly to something risk-related?
- Is there someone in your company that is being sabotaged for risk-taking?
- What would happen if they were empowered to take risks?
- How often do you have difficulty being flexible?
- How often do you get lost in the details?
- How often do you prioritize people as a means to an end?

NOTES

_____

_____

_____

_____

_____

_____

_____

_____

_____

_____

_____

Reflections of
THE CONNECTOR

Are you a Connector?

- In what ways do you exhibit the traits of a Connector?
- What qualities of the Connector do you wish to develop?
- Are there elements of the Connector that feel completely foreign?

Own Your Reputation: The Superpower of Connection

- Does someone in your company have the Superpower to Connect?
- Do any of the mistakes made by other Superpowers resonate with you?

Overcoming the Connector's Blind Spot: Empowerment

- Do you or someone on your team have a blind spot related to empowerment?
- How has this blind spot shaped the relationships within your company?
- Can you think of times when you or someone on your team reacted poorly to a decision that could have impacted your reputation?
- Is someone in your company being sabotaged for taking action without approval?
- What would happen if they were empowered to make decisions?
- How often do you have difficulty staying objective?
- How often do you get lost in the relationship?
- How often do you prioritize appearances over integrity?

NOTES

_____

_____

_____

_____

_____

_____

_____

_____

Reflections of

THE PERSUADER

Are you a Persuader?

- In what ways do you exhibit the traits of a Persuader?
- What qualities of the Persuader do you wish to develop?
- Are there elements of the Persuader that feel completely foreign?

Win Customers: The Superpower of Persuasion

- Does someone in your company have the Superpower to Persuade?
- Do any of the mistakes made by other Superpowers resonate with you?

Overcoming the Persuader's Blind Spot: Consistency

- Do you or someone on your team have a blind spot related to consistency?
- How has this blind spot shaped the relationships within your company?
- Can you think of times when you or someone else on your team tried to enforce consistency?
- Is someone in your company being sabotaged for trying to make things consistent?
- What would happen if they were empowered to keep things consistent?
- How often do you have difficulty with long-term focus?
- How often do you get lost in the deal?
- How often do you prioritize one-off requests?

NOTES

_____

_____

_____

_____

_____

_____

_____

_____

_____

_____

ABOUT THE AUTHOR

Wearing a variety of hats her whole life, Michelle Denogean has an impressive resume. Still, few know that her first ambitious hat had "Writer" written across it. While she has made herself known as a marketing guru and sought-after strategist in the business world, she spent her early years writing short stories and poems and always had a book idea in mind. "My twelve- and thirteen-year-old 'self' wrote many coming-of-age stories," Michelle says. "I had to put my thoughts to paper."

Born and raised in West Hills, California, Michelle kept busy with school, dance, and writing. Always a leader, she was captain of her high school dance team. While she spent her summers working in her father's accounting business, she had zero desire to lead in business. She noticed that her father didn't love what he did career-wise, which kept her away from anything having to do with numbers for a long time.

"I didn't want anything to do with business," she says. "I was a creative, and I thought I would do something that sprung out of my internal creative resources."

She sought and received her bachelor's degree in Communications, with a minor in Literature Writing, from the University of California, San Diego. Throughout her studies, she began to understand the intricacies of business.

With the advent of the highly accessible internet, Michelle began to see that new companies were starting at an all-time high. She saw kids starting businesses out of their garages and people investing millions in them with little to no plan. She thought, "Business is business," and someone would need to be there to pick up the pieces. That led her to Pepperdine University, where she eventually earned her MBA.

She entered the business sector full steam ahead and gained experience in several industries, helping startups achieve scalable success.

With extreme curiosity, Michelle found she could not "stay in her swim lane." Early on, she oversaw Product Development for Fast-click and Analytics and Operations at Edmunds. Over the past fifteen years, she has held the role of Chief Marketing Officer for some of the most successful B2C and B2B brands in the Travel, Automotive and Real Estate industries including Edmunds, Road-ster, Side, and currently, Mindtrip. She also served in leadership positions at eHarmony and Move.com.

Her hard work has paid off. To her delight, in 2023, Michelle received the coveted Icon Award for Top Marketer of the Year.

Combining two of her greatest passions, Michelle knew she would one day write a book about business. "Writing a book was a bucket list item," she explains. "It was originally going to be a fiction one-up until a few years back when I began to get passionate about helping more than just the company I served." That tied in with her reasoning for getting her MBA—she wants to be there for anyone who needs her."

Her inability to stay in the marketing box and her passion for asking provocative questions made her the perfect resource for any-one looking to take their startup to the next level. But she realized she could reach out to many more startup founders with books. With three in the works, she now wears the hat "Author."

Michelle currently resides in Newhall, California, where her husband grew up. They met seventeen years ago at the airport, where both had just returned from business trips. They now have a son and daughter in high school. The family are avid skiers, snowboarders, and off-roaders. Michelle says, "My two wonderful children believe that CMO stands for 'Chief Mommy Officer.'"

Visit Michelle at www.michelledenogean.com

NOTE FROM THE PUBLISHER

BERRY POWELL PRESS
Carmen Berry, Founder
New York Times bestselling author

The privilege of working with someone of Michelle Denogean's level of experience and expertise has been a game changer for us at Berry Powell Press. This book holds a treasured place in my life and career.

As a New York Times bestselling author who signed her first book contract in 1985, I have faced the disappointments and difficulties of navigating the publishing industry. But I also have experienced something only authors can understand—the deep satisfaction of knowing that the hours spent alone working on a manuscript have purpose. The written word has the power to impact the lives of people I will never meet. In 2020, my business partner and I decided it was time to start Berry Powell Press to help other aspiring authors become successful authors.

As *GrowUp* explains, many startups enjoy initial success that can seem unstoppable, even magical. Indeed, the startup team at Berry Powell Press astonished me with their commitment to creative collaboration, which resulted in birthing a new level of author-focused services. It was thrilling.

But then things got harder. What worked before lost its power. I didn't know why. During our third year of operations, the challenges seemed so daunting and confusing that I began to question the sustainability of the original vision—to create a safe place for authors to strive for excellence in their writing and to publish high-end books capable of competing with traditional publishers in content, impact, and quality. Was providing the depth of services I knew authors needed not viable financially?

At that moment in my struggle, Michelle contacted me inquiring about publishing a book to help founders avoid becoming a statistic—part of the ninety percent of startups that fail. She wanted to show founders like me how to transform their startups into successful and sustainable companies. I needed to hear that message at precisely that moment.

I am convinced that Michelle's model in this book clearly defines new companies' challenges. She equips founders to grapple effectively with their strengths, shortcomings, and blind spots. *GrowUp* offers solutions and strategies, plus encouragement when you might want to give up. Why do I believe her message works? Because it is working for me. It has changed the trajectory of Berry Powell Press in a more effective direction.

The values we share at Berry Powell Press are reflected in *GrowUp*: a commitment to excellence, inclusion, compassion, and achievement. We offer this book to those of you who have yet to fulfill the dreams you've harbored for a long time, perhaps even years. If you want to start a new venture that can make the world better, the best place to begin would be reading *GrowUp*. You will be ahead of the other newbies because you'll know what to expect.

If you have already started your company but are struggling to keep the doors open, this is the one book you need to read this year. It will change your paradigm, strategies, and potential success.

If your aspirations include becoming an author, we at Berry Powell would love to meet you.

Visit our website at www.berrypowellpress.com

Berry Powell Press is a hybrid publishing house that publishes authors with transformational perspectives on timely personal and societal challenges. We provide our authors with in-depth mentorship and collaborative assistance to create life-changing books. Additionally, we assist them in building book-based businesses that can impact the largest audience possible. We publish fiction and non-fiction for adults and children.

www.ingramcontent.com/pod-product-compliance
Lightning Source LLC
Chambersburg PA
CBHW060046100426
42742CB00014B/2716